RAJ

A Scrapbook of British India
1877-1947

Charles Allen

PENGUIN BOOKS

Penguin Books Ltd, Harmondsworth,
Middlesex, England
Penguin Books, 625 Madison Avenue,
New York, New York 10022, U.S.A.
Penguin Books Australia Ltd, Ringwood,
Victoria, Australia
Penguin Books Canada Ltd, 2801 John Street,
Markham, Ontario, Canada L3R 1B4
Penguin Books (N.Z.) Ltd, 182–190 Wairau Road,
Auckland 10, New Zealand

First published by André Deutsch Limited 1977
Published in Penguin Books 1979
Text copyright © Charles Allen, 1977
Design copyright © New Leaf Books Limited, 1977

All rights reserved

Designed at New Leaf
2 Motcomb Street, London SW1
Original design conceived by Michael McGuinness
and put into practice by
Malcolm Smythe
With the assistance of Susan Rawkins

Made and printed in Great Britain by
Hazell Watson & Viney Ltd, Aylesbury, Bucks

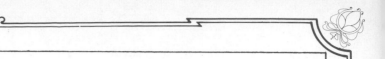

What far-reaching Nemesis steered him
From his home by the cool of the sea?
When he left the fair country that reared him,
When he left her, his Mother, for thee,
That restless, disconsolate worker
Who strains now in vain at thy nets,
O sultry and sombre Noverca!
O Land of Regrets!

Thou has racked him with duns and diseases,
And he lies, as thy scorching winds blow,
Recollecting old England's sea breezes,
On his back in a lone bungalow;
At the slow coming darkness repining
How he girds at the sun till it sets,
As he marks the long shadows declining
O'er the Land of Regrets

The Land of Regrets
Sir Alfred Lyall, 1885

❧ Contents ❧

Acknowledgements

In *Plain Tales from the Raj* I drew upon the recorded experiences of a number of men and women who had lived and worked in India in the last years of the Raj. For this scrapbook I have tried to develop my own impressions of that era in visual terms, going back further in time so as to include the earlier days of British India and drawing more heavily on those families whose connections with India very often date back to the days of the East India Company.

That very Victorian institution of the scrapbook was essentially an informal family record and in keeping with this sense of family – so very important in British India with its long tradition of service – I have chosen the bulk of my material from private rather than from public sources and have given preference to amateur rather than to professional illustrations. Where there have been gaps I have tried to fill these from what were once private (and still, I hope, unfamiliar) albums and scrapbooks in public hands.

My principal thanks must be to those remarkable families and their descendants, who offered me most valuable advice and assistance and, in some cases, unlimited use of their family albums and papers, in particular, Joan and Geoffrey Allen; E. C. Armitage, Esq; Henry Bannerman, Esq; Nicolas Bentley, Esq; Vere, Lady Birdwood; Ted Brown, Esq; Mrs Veronica Burnett; Bill Catto, Esq; Col. Henry and Mrs Cotton; Sir John and Lady Cotton; Mrs Sheila Craven; Eric and Irene Edwards; John Hearsey, Esq; W. F. Harvey, Esq; Maj. E. S. Humphries; J. W. Inglis, Esq; Les Jasper, Esq; Mrs Angela Macey; Col. Kenneth Mason; Col. J. K. La Touche Mardon; Rupert Mayne, Esq; Mrs Iris Portal; John Rivett-Carnac, Esq; Sir Reginald Savory; Sir John Smyth; Sir Herbert Stewart; Nancy and Raymond Vernède; Mr and Mrs M. Watney; and others whose help was offered, but could not always be taken.

In addition to these private individuals I would also like to thank the following persons and organizations for their assistance: Lt-Col V. W. Tregear, Editor of the *Piffer* magazine; B. C. Bloomfield, Paul Fox and library staff at the School of Oriental and African Studies; the Council for World Mission; the Baptist Missionary Society; Dr Richard Bingle and staff at the India Office Library; Dr Boris Mollo and staff at the National Army Museum; the Army and Navy Stores; P & O; the National Maritime Museum; the Cambridge Centre of South Asian Studies; James Fraser of Gordon Fraser Books. Finally, my special thanks to Henry Nelson, Director of the British in India Museum at Colne (an institution that deserves the support of all those interested in preserving the detail of social life in British India), and to my colleague, Sean Sprague, for his help in photo-research and photography.

CHARLES ALLEN   London, 1977

'Outdoor relief for Britain's upper classes': although not quite
as *pukka* as Probyn's Horse, otherwise known as the 'Hindu
Blues' on account of its aristocratic connections, the
outstanding regiment in India was the Guides Cavalry and
Infantry.

Introduction

'Remember Cawnpore': the memorial well at Cawnpore, with its sculptured angel by Baron Marochetti, was British India's most sacred monument.
'Remember Cawnpore', scrawled on the walls of the *bibi khana* where over two hundred women and children were slaughtered in July 1857, remained a powerful rallying-cry among the British for years to come. Until shortly before World War II Indians were forbidden to enter Cawnpore's Memorial Gardens.

The British occupation of India lasted just less than two centuries; two contrasting periods of rule bloodily divided by that long summer of horrors known as the Indian Mutiny. The first century was one of rapid expansion as the British 'conquered and peopled half the world in a fit of absence of mind.' With the help of its youthful conquistadores – the Clives, Clevelands, Malcolms, Lawrences, Nicholsons and other warrior-administrators of the same mould – the British East India Company (known familiarly as 'John Company') learned to match and then to master oriental custom. By treaty, bribery, annexation and open conquest it spread its commercial empire north from Madras to Bengal and then westwards across upper India and into the Punjab. By the summer of 1857 three-fifths of the sub-continent lay under its control.

The self-confidence of the British in India had never been higher. They saw this as a golden age and themselves as agents of Western enlightenment. By contrast, the self-confidence of the Indians was at its lowest. The appetite of John Company both for change and for further conquest seemed insatiable. A reaction was inevitable and when it came its ferocity was perhaps as much a surprise to the Indians themselves as it was to the British communities scattered far and wide across the Indian landscape.

The suppression of the Mutiny took a year and a half of bitter fighting and the wounds it left behind were never healed. It forced the two communities apart and created a Mutiny mentality – a refusal to trust the Indian – that the British in India never quite shook off. In England it was seen as an event so shocking and so thrilling that it became the great romance of the Victorian age, an epic complete with such stern heroes as Henry Lawrence, John Nicholson and Henry Havelock, perfectly suited to the gothic sentimentality of that era. Lucknow, Cawnpore and Delhi, where the fiercest fighting took place, were no longer just place names; they were now keynotes in the litany of the British Empire. In India itself Cawnpore, with its dreadful history of massacre upon massacre, acquired something of the status of a cult among the British, justifying their presence, warranting their caution. No scrapbook was complete without its Marochetti angel.

The Mutiny marked the beginnings of modern India. On 1 November 1858, at a cold and spiritless Durbar at Allahabad presided over by its first Viceroy, the Raj rose from the ashes of John Company. Government by commercial enterprise now gave way to crown rule, with an Indian Civil Service, a restructured Indian Army and matching reforms in law, finance, land systems and education.

The Viceroy's map now showed two Indias, a patchwork of imperial pink and princely yellow. In the west there were the arid provinces of Baluchistan and Sind, separated from the rest of British India by a belt of native states running from the deserts of Rajputana to the Eastern Ghats. In Southern India there were the Central Provinces and the two Presidencies of Bombay and Madras, divided from each other by the native states of Mysore and Hyderabad. In the east there was the Bengal Presidency (later to be fatally partitioned by Lord Curzon into East and West Bengal), and the province of Assam – soon to be joined by Burma. Running north-west from Bengal there was a solid line of British provinces that formed the backbone of British India: Bihar, the United Provinces, the Punjab and, in due course, the North-West Frontier Province. These ten provinces of British India and the 562 native states that made up the 'real' India now went their separate ways, sharing only a common allegiance to the Crown in the person of the Viceroy.

In the native states a bejewelled diversity of Nizams, Maharajahs, Rajas, Mehtars, Ranas, Raos, Ackonds, Jams, Walis and other lesser salute princes – each with his own entitlement to gun salutes that rose according to status by odd numbers from nine to twenty-one – were left to rule very much as they pleased. At one end of the scale there was Hyderabad, as large as England and Scotland put together, and at the other a handful of petty chiefdoms each with a few dusty acres of land. Some of these men, like the Maharajahs of Bikaner and Patiala, chose to govern as thoroughly enlightened rulers; a few reverted to feudal barbarism. The great majority continued to mark time, fending off as far as possible the advice of the British Residents or Political Agents that were stationed in their domains.

In British India the Raj was personified by the Collector or Deputy Commissioner, known to his critics first as the 'competition-*wallah*' and later as the 'heaven-born' – an allusion, made partly in jest and partly in earnest, to the Brahmin, highest of the four principal castes in the Hindu social order. As one of the new breed of covenanted Indian Civil Servants (ICS) who governed by the pen rather than the sword, he administered a District as large, on average, as Norfolk, with a population probably well in excess of a million. To support him he had a brace or two of Assistants and a range of supporting services that ran from the Superintendent of Police by way of the Public Works Engineer or the Sub-Divisional

H.H. The Maharaja of Orcha.

A very average princely autocrat: Sir Pratap Singh Bahadur ruled a small central Indian state of some two thousand square miles. As a personal mark of favour, Lord Curzon increased his gun salute from fifteen to seventeen.

Forest Officer to Inspectors of Opium and Sub-Inspectors of Posts and Telegraphs. Together, in the 250 Districts of British India, he and his colleagues saw to it that Pax Britannica prevailed over the 2,300 recognized castes, sects and creeds that made up the civil population.

The way in which these officials and others of their kind – in the Army and in a variety of occupations – lived and worked under the Raj forms the subject of this present scrapbook. The 'tale of their lives' has been told often enough, their papers have been worked over, their recorded voices have been assembled and edited. But visual records of their lives are limited.

The greater part of what was once preserved in albums, scrapbooks and private papers has been lost; much of it was thrown away in the years that followed Indian independence in 1947. Much of that way of life never found a place in a photograph album or a sketch-book and must be left to the imagination; the scene in a Sub-Divisional Magistrate's court, for instance, as it must have been in the Hot Weather, packed with sweating humanity, stifling, closely shuttered against the sun, with the presiding magistrate delivering a judgement in the vernacular in a case concerning the trespass of a cow, knowing full well that both sides and their hired witnesses had perjured themselves. Such scenes were indeed the essence of the Raj; yet enough remains to give us at least a flavour of a vanished way of life and some idea of why it was so especially remarkable.

After the Mutiny it took the best part of two decades for the Raj to form and settle but once the style of the period had been struck – by 1877 or thereabouts – very little changed, either in physical terms or in terms of attitude and behaviour. This quite extraordinary cohesiveness is one of the most distinctive features of the Raj.

If a well-seasoned sahib or 'old *koi-hai*' had stepped out of the pages of Sir Henry Cunningham's *Chronicles of Dustypore* (a popular novel about life in an up-country station) or Phil Robinson's *In My Indian Garden* (which started a vogue in light satirical sketches of Indian life), both published in 1877, and into an up-country bungalow in 1937, he would have been surprised only by the short skirts of the memsahib and the diminished quantity of servants. The structure of the bungalow would not have changed. It was the same spartan, functional dwelling built by amateur architects with limited resources, still never lived in long enough to seem like a real home.

In many out-stations he could still have dined by lamplight with a *pull-punkah* swinging overhead (although, if there had been a loyal toast, he would have drunk to the King-Emperor rather than the Queen-Empress), still have sprawled out after dinner on a verandah 'long-sleever' (but with a *chota peg* of whisky or even a 'gimlet' in his hand rather than a brandy), still washed in a hip-bath in the *gussal-khana*, and still slept under a mosquito net. In the corner of his room a piano might still have been found with its legs in saucers of water – to keep off white ants – another saucer inside the piano containing quicklime so as to absorb excessive moisture.

The books by his bedside would have changed but he would have found their subject matter agreeably familiar. The Indian romances and Mutiny novels of Flora Annie Steel and Maud Diver would almost certainly have been well represented, as well as Kipling's *Plain Tales*, *Ditties* and *Ballads* and such classic Anglo-Indian satires as Aberigh-Mackay's *Twenty-One Days in India*, *Lays of Ind* by 'Aliph Cheem', *Tribes on My Frontier* and *Behind the Bungalow* by 'EHA' – all of them published in the 1880s and 1890s. There would have been books on horses (probably by Captain Hayes) and books on *shikar* (hunting and shooting) with such titles as *Thirteen Years Among the Wild Beasts of India* or *With Rod and Gun in the Hindu Koh*. There would certainly have been a copy of *The Complete Indian Housekeeper and Cook* ('We do not wish to advocate an unholy haughtiness; but an Indian household can no more be governed peacefully, without dignity and prestige, than an Indian Empire'), and very probably an old friend, Dr Moore's *Family Medicine*, which was first published in 1874 and ran into nine reprints and was always – like so much else in British India – a decade or so behind the times.

The old *koi-hai* would certainly have frowned at the general air of undress that had crept in since the Great War. Yet even here a long tradition of unsuitability was maintained often with tight, starched and heavy clothing frequently worn on duty or in the evening, and the compulsive business of flannel or wool next to the skin ('woollen clothing, thick or thin, should be the clothing of a child all the year round'). Perhaps it had something to do with pride – a refusal to 'go native' – something to do with the feeling that every Englishman from the Governor's ADC to the planter's assistant shared of being permanently on show. It was also inextricably bound up with a refusal to move with the times: 'Wear a sun hat till sunset,' advised the official *Notes for Officers proceeding to India*. 'To protect the neck, a *topi* with a good long extension is necessary. But, as the spine itself has to be protected, it is best in very hot weather to wear a padded spinal pad, made to hook on to the outside of the coat and provided with small cork wads to make an air space between coat and pad.' This was issued not, as one might reasonably suppose, in the 1880s but a full fifty years later.

This enduring timelessness had come about through a combination of circumstances which came to fruition at about the time of the Great Durbar, held on 1 January 1877, to mark the proclamation of Queen Victoria as Empress of India. In 1876-7 famine was devastating South India and for the first time serious action was being taken to combat its effects. The Second Afghan War was about to break out, with another military catastrophe (at Maiwand) and another little victory (Roberts' march on Kandahar) soon to complete the picture. Rudyard Kipling would soon be sailing out to join his father in Lahore. Lord Lytton was Viceroy: a vain, romantic, brilliant statesman who shocked Anglo-Indian society by smoking between courses at dinner and who had much in common with two other outstanding Viceroys of this era, Curzon (whose Viceroyalty marked the high point of the Raj), and Mountbatten (who brought it abruptly to a close).

By 1877 two great advances in engineering had begun radically to alter the shape of things in India. Lacing and drawing together every corner of the sub-continent was a railway system that was now uniting India as never before. Begun just too late to halt the Mutiny at its outset, the railways would be all but completed by the turn of the century. Even when slowed to suit the pace of India, eight major railway systems operating on five different gauges soon made it possible to travel in comfort from Peshawar on the North-West Frontier to Tuticorin in

1 January 1877, when the Raj came of age: the first Delhi Durbar, at which Queen Victoria was proclaimed *Kaiser-i-Hind*, Queen-Empress of India

the south, in days rather than weeks. Troops and food-grains as well as passengers could now be moved quickly from province to province. India had become an altogether smaller place.

Even more significant was the opening of the Suez Canal in 1869, drawing India and England some five thousand miles closer and turning an upredictable voyage of up to six months into a four-week passage where the mail could be relied upon to arrive at Bombay on Friday morning and depart on Saturday night. Yet the narrowing of the geographical distance could only widen the emotional gap between the two races. As communications improved, so India became less and less a land of exile to which one was inexorably committed for better or worse. It became possible to go home on furlough every few years and to bring out wives and daughters – just as it was now possible to avoid the worst of the Hot Weather by catching a train to the Hills.

The male-orientated British India of pre-Mutiny days had gone and the Anglo-India of Kipling's Mrs Hauksbee and the Gadsbys had arrived. By her mere presence the memsahib placed a new barrier between her sahib and the land, while the sahibs themselves – who had once called themselves 'Indians' and had Indianized in a variety of ways that ranged from taking native wives or *bibis* to wearing pyjamas and smoking *hubble-bubble* pipes – now drew in upon

themselves, reinforcing their own identity as 'Anglo-Indians'. Against the all-consuming, debilitating breadth of the Indian landscape the urge to strengthen and defend had become almost instinctive. 'A man should, whatever happens, keep to his own caste, race and breed,' urges the young Kipling in the opening of one of his grimmer *Plain Tales from the Hills*, reflecting the sentiments of this new age.

In building up their own identity the Anglo-Indians also set themselves further apart from their fellow-countrymen back home. What could anyone in England hope to make of a world that was bounded by civil stations and hill stations; a world of Governor's Camps, gymkhanas, Gloom Clubs, Black Hearts and Cold Weather tours; of walers, hog spears, Roorkee chairs and bedding rolls; of Curzon topees, Bombay bowlers, spine-pads and belly-bands; of Piffers, Orders of Precedence, the *Pioneer*, the C *and* M, the PVH and the KCIE? It was not an order of existence that English cousins could easily relate to.

This double isolation did much to fix Anglo-Indian attitudes, preserving, to the point of exaggeration, standards and norms of behaviour long after the same attitudes had been abandoned elsewhere. But the net result of this hardening of attitudes was not the hidebound 'little England' mentality that one might have expected. What emerged was a heightened sense of moral righteousness which, at its worst, produced the bully and the racist, the types who habitually called all Indians 'niggers' (later, 'wogs') and mocked and disparaged all things Indian. At its best, this same righteousness gave India a ruling elite of Englishmen and Scotsmen that was second to none. With 'duty' and 'service' as its watchwords, it demanded a commitment to India so total as to border on the obsessive.

If the cohesiveness of the Raj had grown out of isolation it was maintained by exclusiveness. At its heart was a tradition of family service kept up by a relatively small but closely inter-connected number of families – Bayleys, Birdwoods, Cottons, Cunninghams, Grants, Rivett-Carnacs, Trevelyans and other less well-known names – whose sons followed their fathers for as many as five or six generations, the eldest son trying for the Indian Civil Service, the second for the Indian Army or the police and so on. Some families tended to specialize, concentrating on one particular occupation or joining 'family' regiments. Nine members of the Cotton family were represented in the Civil or Political Services between 1762 and 1947. Three Durands – Algernon, Edward and Henry – served in the political service on the North-West Frontier, following in the footsteps of their father, General Sir H. M. Durand (whose celebrated death at Tonk in 1871 – when the elephant on which he was travelling went under an arch that was too low for its passenger – passed into the folklore of Anglo-India). At about the time of the Great War three Osmastons (father, brother and son) could be found in the Indian Forest Service. Intermarriage between these Anglo-Indian families strengthened the commitment to India, building up within a couple of generations a semi-exclusive caste, the 'Brahmins' of British India.

In terms of class, the social structure of British India was unique. The British penetration of India in the eighteenth century had provided, as a contemporary observer noted, 'a vast system of outdoor relief for Britain's upper classes', chiefly for the younger sons of the country gentry – sons of the manse from Scotland and Ulster, in particular – who found in India a means of restoring their family fortunes without losing their status. In time this aristocracy of working gentlemen formed itself into 'official' India, and was made up of civil and military officers.

The old East India Company had always guarded its Indian monopoly jealously, and something of this prejudice against 'interlopers' lingered on amongst 'officials' after the Mutiny, making it difficult for those of humbler origin to gain a foothold for themselves within India. Those who managed to set themselves up as merchants or traders were known disparagingly as box-*wallahs* (pedlars) and were never fully accepted, however rich they became. No place was ever found for them in the Orders of Precedence that were used to establish just who was senior to whom and who sat where at the *burra khana* (dinner party). Rudyard Kipling's patron, a wealthy newspaper magnate named George Allen, had started business in India in the 1850s as a chemist. Forty years later 'Anglo-Indian society, though quite ready to eat his expensive dinners, drink his expensive wines, and accept his costly presents, would not fraternise with anyone who had been in trade. In this respect it was far more select than royalty.'

These two widely-separated classes – the officials and the mercantile community – constituted Anglo-India, leaving very little room for the British working classes, who came to India chiefly as birds of passage. Yet large numbers of British working men did come to know India, even if only briefly and under severe restrictions. For well over a century and a half the British Army made India its second home, bringing out regiment after regiment to serve its turn in some dusty, isolated cantonment. But Tommy Atkins was never made welcome; British India did its best to ignore his presence.

Missionaries also found themselves to be outsiders. Their predecessors had for some decades been actively prevented from entering British territories in India, and later on their excessive zeal had played a part in bringing on the Mutiny. Thereafter they found a more useful place for themselves as educators and medical workers midway between the two communities. If they had no real place in Anglo-Indian society it was partly by their own choice.

Much less fortunate were the offspring of mixed marriages and liaisons between English men and Indian women. Some of these families, like the Gardners and the Hearseys, were descendants of the 'best' families on both sides. Even so, they came to be regarded as tainted by mixed blood and were lumped beyond the pale, so to speak, together with other Eurasians and 'poor whites' (known colloquially as 'country breds'). Certain occupations, chiefly on the railways and in lower provincial appointments, were allotted to them but unless they were educated overseas all the senior and covenanted posts were barred. In 1900 they were officially designated 'Anglo-Indians' but Anglo-India preferred to keep the title for itself and simply went on calling them Eurasians.

The predominance of the upper classes gave great scope to what might be termed the public school spirit. India was, if not exactly won, then certainly run on the playing fields of Eton – where over half its Viceroys were educated – to say nothing of Haileybury and Wellington and other such hearty institutions. Custom demanded, partly for reasons of health, partly because of the corrupting influence of Indian morals ('the evil influence of native servants'), that all children be sent Home to be educated, so between the ages of five and seven they were packed off to exile in a strange and rather dull country, to draw what comfort they could from the disciplines of boarding-school. If they returned to India, they came back with that curious mixture of sheltered innocence and self-confidence that is the hallmark of the English public school education.

They also came out as natural conservatives, very often as strangers to their parents but with a close affinity to the land of their birth. They believed in fair play, in supporting the under-dog and in hard and fast prefectorial attitudes that allowed no room for lies or deceit or disloyalty. They remained seniors in charge of juniors, paternalists at heart. 'It does not follow that we are always necessarily right,' states 'J.E.D.' in his *Notes on an Outfit for India and Hints for the New Arrival,* published in 1903. 'It is true, however, that we are nearly always far more practical; hence the need for us in the country. The most experienced and best natured of our countrymen agree in comparing the uneducated natives of India to children, who themselves fully admit the justice of the description, for they commonly appeal to their masters as "my father and mother".'

Ultimately, of course, their loyalty was to their own kind; rather than let the side down they would oppose innovation, profess to being anti-intellectual

John Rivett-Carnac joined the Indian Police in 1909. His father was Deputy Inspector-General of Police in Bengal, his grandfather was a judge in Dacca at the time of the Mutiny, his great-grandfather a Governor of Bombay, his great-great-grandfather a General in the Bengal Army at the time of Clive.

and behave with open philistinism towards such unmanly pursuits as music or art – especially if these were Indian. Such blind loyalty found its greatest expression in the regimental messes of the Indian Army. Here team spirit was everything; nothing could be allowed to stand in the way of the regiment and its honour. Whether his men were Punjabi Mussulmans, Dogras, Jats, Madrassis, Mahrattas, Baluchis, Sikhs or Gurkhas, every officer found in them some special quality that set them apart from and above the rest.

One of the ironies of the Indian Mutiny had been the way in which colonel after colonel had insisted that he knew his men, that *his* regiment – so steeped in tradition and regimental esprit – would remain loyal. In a way, they did – but not always to their officers. Even after the Mutiny the British officer's faith in his *jawans* (young warriors – the word *sepoy* rather lost its flavour after 1857), sentimental and naive as it was, remained utterly sincere. The *jawan* responded in turn with a devotion to the regiment that was absolute. The word that they had for it was *bhai-bundi,* which might loosely be rendered as brotherhood.

The young subaltern who joined an Indian regiment had perhaps the easiest introduction to India that anyone could possibly hope for, since he moved by comfortable stages from school to Sandhurst (Woolwich, if he was a Gunner; Chatham, if he was a Royal Engineer), from there to a British regiment stationed in India and from the British regiment to whichever Indian regiment would take him. Although hunting rather than sporting trophies hung on the walls of the mess, its chummy all-male atmosphere was familiar to him. Here he lived in a self-contained world where he was sheltered and – except for infrequent bouts of active service – pampered. In return he was required to give the regiment his unswerving support and to share its beliefs and unspoken prejudices.

Those outside the army could expect to have a rather harsher introduction to India. First contracts were always the longest, with terms that weeded out faint-hearts, misfits and the poor in health. Up to the Great War, four or five unbroken years before one's first leave was very much the norm, usually served out in remote up-country stations. The Punjab and the United Provinces headed the list as the most sought-after provinces but the less fortunate found themselves posted to the Sind desert or the jungles of Upper Burma. Wherever they went to, these newcomers to India – known in Victorian times as 'griffins' – could expect to find themselves isolated and dependent for comfort and advice on Indian subordinates. They shouldered immediate responsibility and picked up the job as they went along. In such situations young men matured quickly – and learned to follow precedent. If the nearest European happened to be one's immediate superior, the local 'burra sahib' – and he very often was – then it was difficult not to follow his example. 'Now these are the laws of the jungle,' wrote Rudyard Kipling, Anglo-India's undisputed poet laureate, 'and many and mighty are they! But the head and the hoof and the haunch and the hump is – Obey!'

This first exposure to India had one other far-reaching effect. The European became immediately conscious that he was a member of the dominant race and that he and his kind were scattered far and thin across the land. The ICS, for instance, was only a thousand strong at the turn of the century; a ratio of four civil officers to every million Indians. Its prestige was enormous and had to remain so if it was to continue to claim respect and obedience. Every Englishman in India benefited from this prestige and was expected to uphold it in return. There was to be no rocking of the boat or, as early editions of Bradshaw's *Handbooks to the Presidencies* put it: 'The moral behaviour of all classes of

Major Wigram Battye, paladin of the Guides, killed leading a cavalry charge during the Second Afghan War, 1879. An elder brother died leading the Guides against the mutineers at Delhi in 1857, a younger brother during the relief of Chitral in 1895. A fourth brother in the Guides survived into the twentieth century.

Europeans should be extremely discreet, not only to preserve that inestimable blessing, health, but to command the respect of the native community.'

Wealth and conspicuous living had little place in the life-style of the Raj but custom, as much Indian as Anglo-Indian, decreed that the *lat* sahib (lord and master) should maintain certain standards. Such official or semi-official dicta as 'every officer shall keep a charger' or 'officers only travel in first-class carriages' forced many younger men to spend their first decades in India in debt or carefully disguised poverty. Early marriages were rare – indeed, some contracts went so far as to cite matrimony as grounds for immediate dismissal, and at the very least, permission from the *burra* sahib was required. The result was that men married late, and married couples often showed a marked disparity in their ages. This was particularly evident during the Victorian era, which might well account for the atmosphere of 'duty and red tape, picnics and adultery' that was sometimes said to characterize Simla in the last decades of the nineteenth century.

With each promotion the sahib drew a little closer to the centre, from the outlying sub-division to the centre of the district, from the district to the provincial capital, from there to Calcutta or (after 1911) to New Delhi. At each step salaries increased and conditions became less arduous, with a wider range of comforts on hand – better hired furniture to choose from, electric fans instead of *punkahs*, a local cold store and perhaps a mutton or beef 'club', a bigger and better gymkhana club providing a greater choice of sporting activities, the means to buy and support a second string for polo and so play twice as many *chukkas*, more entertaining and entertainment, more European faces. Conversely, there were fewer encounters with Indians, more reliance on intermediaries, rather more abstract and rather less first-hand knowledge.

Only in the last years – with an early retirement and a good pension ahead of him – could the sahib really afford to live well. He was now a *pukka burra sahib* and his wife very probably a *sakt* (tough) *burra mem*. Whether he was Chief Magistrate, Colonel of the Regiment, Conservator of Forests in Bihar or Orissa or something important in the Secretariat, the Railways Board, the Central Bank or the Calcutta head office, he was, without a shadow of doubt, a power in the land. The senior clubs opened their doors to him. Governors asked him to dine and presented him to touring Viceroys. He who had once modelled himself on great and mighty *burra* sahibs was now himself a model for others. The continuity was not broken. Only one more powerful social obligation remained to be fulfilled: custom required that he keep open house, entertaining guests – notably his junior colleagues – most nights of the week, and make at least an appearance at every social function. He retired early; there were very few old Englishmen in India.

There was really no place for women in the first of these three stages of Anglo-Indian man. That first formative connection with the land and its people was kept from them, making it almost inevitable that they should remain always at a certain distance from the real India. The luckiest were the girls who had known India in their early childhood and who returned to it as if returning home. They came out in their late teens, sailing out early in the autumn at the start of the Cold Weather. Other girls came with them, innocent young ladies who knew nothing of India but had invitations to stay with an uncle or a distant relative for the 'season'.

In mid-October the Cold Weather was officially stated to have begun, government allowances for *punkah-wallahs* were stopped and there was an overnight change from summer to winter clothing. Off came the topees and on went the trilbies and 'double *terais*'. There followed – for the young unmarried women – four months of concentrated gaiety, crowded with tea-dances, club dances, dinner dances, fancy-dress balls, moonlight picnics, gymkhanas, polo weeks, Civil Service weeks, garden parties, Governor's Camps, Viceregal balls. It may well have been a marvellous marriage-market but it can hardly have given a more distorted picture of the realities of Anglo-Indian life.

The bachelor who failed to find himself a bride amidst the stiff competition of the Cold Weather season went Home in search of one. The wife he returned with can have had little inkling of the kind of life she was expected to lead. Once her husband had left the bungalow in the morning she was alone, surrounded by servants with whom she could not communicate and by a complexity of Indian conventions – summed up in the word *dastur* – 'the stifling, enervating atmosphere of custom, against which energy beats itself unavailingly, as against a feather bed' – that far exceeded anything Anglo-India could come up with. She had precious little alternative but to turn to other memsahibs and adopt their standards.

It has often been said that all the worst faults of the Raj – its petty intolerance, its prejudices and snobberies, its cold-hearted arrogance – stemmed from the memsahib. The fact of the matter is that the memsahib never really stood much of a chance – and the wonder is that so many came through so well. Consider the wives of the regiment, for example, the majority of whom knew about regimental

18

esprit only by hearsay and were never allowed to share in its more primitive rituals: giving away the prizes at inter-company hockey matches but never really knowing the men around whom their husbands built their lives, never even entering that holy of holies, the officers' mess (except, in later years, on rare ladies' nights). They faced months of boredom and loneliness while their husbands were away on active service, years when their children were away and growing up into strangers. Small wonder that they made what they could of their privileges and their pleasures.

Ironically, praise was always lavished on those exceptional wives who stood by their husbands through thick and thin, who stayed behind in the plains in the Hot Weather when they might have been flirting with subalterns in the Hills, who chose not to go Home with the children and see them through school, who took off into the *mofussil* (interior) when their husbands went on tour, living in tents and putting up with curried game every day. Yet in many ways these were the lucky ones, who saw something of their husbands' India, who shared the pride and satisfaction to be got from working through the worst that India could throw at you, in pushing through some irrigational canal or dry weather road against every kind of obstacle, in damping down that smouldering local insubordination. The day's work offered extraordinary challenges to ordinary men, adding dimensions to their lives they could not have found elsewhere – and perhaps it was this single factor that lay at the root of the British determination to see it through.

'The sacredness of India haunts me like a passion,' declared England's greatest propagandist of Empire, George Nathaniel Curzon. 'To me the message is carved in granite, hewn in the rock of doom: that our work is righteous and that it shall endure.' During the six years of his viceroyalty (1899-1905) the patterns of the Raj found their supreme expression: 'It is only when you get to see and realize what India really is – that she is the strength and greatness of England – it is only then that you feel that every nerve a man may strain, every energy he may put forward cannot be devoted to a nobler purpose than keeping tight the cords that hold India to ourselves.'

Nothing could show that nerve and energy more splendidly than Curzon's Great Durbar of 1903, which marked the high noon of Empire in a blaze of power and spectacle. This was to be the very zenith of the Raj. The Great War changed much, but not until the 30s did the cords that held India really

Memsahib in rickshaw, South India, *c*. 1895: 'A new barrier between the sahib and the land . . . '

begin to slacken. For all their professed intentions, those in power shared it only when forced to do so. They gave way with great reluctance, step by step, like parents unwilling to recognize that their offspring had grown up and had no further need of them. When the final break came in 1947 it was swift and total – again, almost as much a surprise to both parties as the Indian Mutiny ninety years before. It was as if those who had been holding on to India for so long had suddenly lost heart and let go.

The Raj had established peace, unity, law and order and stability – perhaps too much stability. It brought with it a foreign people who were, in their own curious way, wary of India and yet loved it. Not always in the right way, perhaps, and not always doing what was best for India, but at least supposing that they were. India gave them rare opportunities; some of them seized their chances, many failed. By and large, they meant well.

19

A British trooper passing through the Suez Canal at the turn
of the century. Before the opening of the canal the fastest
means of getting to and from India was by taking the
overland route through Egypt from Alexandria to Suez,
travelling by camel across the desert.

1

Coming Out: Voyages and Travels

The sea voyage to India was a very necessary period of quarantine between two quite different spheres of existence. For the passengers on the great fleets of liners that plied between Europe and the East it was a last chance to relax and enjoy themselves among their own kind before confronting the rigours and responsibilities that lay ahead. For those new to the East it gave them time to adjust, to observe and to gather advice from more experienced passengers as, by gradual degrees of latitude and longitude, they moved away from a rather staid, regularized way of life and drew closer to a world of bewildering contrasts, where almost everything – whether it was distance, light, darkness, heat or cold – went by extremes.

The East began not at Suez but at Port Said where, on 'baggage day', all the luggage marked 'Wanted on Voyage' (containing tropical wear) was exchanged for the luggage marked 'Cabin' (containing cold weather wear). Double awnings were now erected over most of the deck. 'It is not prudent to go ashore at Port Said in European head gear,' declares 'J.E.D.' in his *Notes on an Outfit*; while the *Notes for Officers proceeding to India* adds another dimension to the mysterious East with the warning that 'at this port you can only land from a trooper in uniform and with a revolver. Be very careful of men who want to sell or show you "French photographs".'

After the slow drift down the Canal (more energetic travellers could take a side trip across the desert to Cairo and the Pyramids and catch the boat up at Suez) there was one more port of call, at Aden for coaling, before the last run across the Indian ocean. Distinctions of caste and career – different ties, subtle variations of evening wear (white dinner jackets with dark trousers worn by those from the Punjab, vice versa for those from Bengal), different group-

ings, increasing aloofness – became accentuated as passengers prepared themselves for India.

The initial impact of the sub-continent was always dramatic: ferocious sun, dazzling sunlight, broad, shimmering landscapes and intoxicating scents, riots of sound and movement and primary colours. Thereafter the process of familiarization continued at a gentler pace as the traveller proceeded up-country. By the 1880s the discomfort of travelling by *palkee* (palanquin) – jolting day and night across the land on the shoulders of four men at a steady five miles an hour – was already becoming a thing of the past with hundreds of miles of new railway track being laid across the sub-continent every year.

The railways were the new lifelines of India, run with model efficiency by European Traffic Superintendents and their Eurasian subordinates and accommodating every possible class of passenger from first to third, by way of second and intermediate – with additional compartments for women and for servants. They were run as public companies, with the two largest – the GIP (Great Indian Peninsular) and the BB and CI (Bombay, Baroda and Central India) – engaging in considerable rivalry as they competed for the Delhi traffic. First-class fares were expensive – about ten times the cost of third-class travel – but they subsidized rail travel for the majority of the railway's users, making it genuinely available to everybody. Only occasionally were there discordant features: 'Indians are fully entitled to travel in first-class carriages if they pay the fare,' warns *Notes for Officers*. 'You are not entitled to demand to see their tickets. Indians often bring strange things into the compartment but anything about which you can really complain is rare. In no case must violence be resorted to.'

21

THE ACCEPTED WAY

OVER the waters of the Eastern Hemisphere, the accepted way for travellers is by the P. & O. and British India Lines. Since 1918, in replacement of war losses and other tonnage, the Companies have newly added to their fleets modern, beautifully appointed passenger vessels of 8,000 to 22,000 tons, amounting, all told, to 533,826 tons gross, or, including newly-added cargo vessels, 894,138 tons gross.

To travel P. & O. is to travel without trouble—with supreme assurance of comfort and attention, and with a personal service that is unequalled.

Regard for those who desire inexpensive, practical comfort has led to the institution of the P. & O. "Tourist Class" in certain vessels on the route, Europe—India—Australia and ports between. Particulars on application.

P&O and BRITISH INDIA LINES

The Exile's Line. The Peninsular and Oriental Steam Navigation Company was always reckoned to be the smartest of lines; it was the oldest, it carried the mails and it never took dogs on board. Travellers to Madras and Calcutta – as well as dog-lovers – generally went on Bibby and British India boats. Ellerman's City and Hall Lines and Lloyd Triestino were comparative latecomers to the field. Passengers travelling first class on P & O ships received free pocket-books, containing useful information about the voyage. If they were experienced travellers they avoided the sun by booking cabins on the port side going out and starboard side coming home – travelling 'POSH' (Port Out, Starboard Home).

S.S. "Worcestershire" off Suez 5.5.11

BIBBY LINE

To the dear Sea Boy a picture of mummy's steamer with much love

Girls of the 'Fishing Fleet', 1913. The term originated early in the nineteenth century when unmarried women were regularly shipped out in batches to meet the demand for wives. In later years the phrase referred to the girls who came out at the beginning of the Cold Weather with friends or relatives. Those who returned without husbands or fiancés were known as 'Returned Empties'.

The perils of the Bay of Biscay could be avoided by travelling across France by train and catching up the boat at Marseilles. An even shorter voyage could be made by taking a Lloyd Triestino ship from Brindisi.

LUNCHEON.

Solferino Soup. Fried Fish.
Orly Sauce. Mutton Cutlets.
and Green Peas. Prawn Curry.
Cold Roast Lamb. Mint Sauce
Cold Roast Ribs Beef.
Sheeps Trotters. Saute
Potatoes. Salad. Cheese.
Tapioca Pudding. Queen
Cakes. Dessert. Coffee.

P. & O. S.S. "SOUDAN"
May 23rd 1903.

With passenger lists very largely made up of unaccompanied men and women, shipboard romances flourished. In other respects the usual proprieties were strictly observed. Passengers were not expected to don tropical wear before they reached the Suez Canal. Here a complete change of wardrobe was made: white drill suits replaced ordinary suits and the black cummerbund replaced the waistcoat whilst the topee took over from the trilby.

Fancy dress aboard a Lloyd Triestino vessel in 1925. A notable feature of station life in British India, the fancy-dress ball was also the high point of the voyage out and was taken so seriously that a complete fancy-dress outfit was a regular part of the traveller's trousseau.

Dressing for dinner began with the sounding of the dressing-gong one hour before the first sitting. During dinner a succession of gongs were sounded to mark the arrival of each course, giving passengers a chance to miss the early courses. Older travellers preferred the second sitting, which gave them greater opportunity to honour the Anglo-Indian custom of drinking before rather than after meals.

Ladies' egg and spoon race, from a P & O postcard, 1908. To lighten the monotony numerous deck-games were organized. A daily feature of the voyage was the lottery based on the ship's run, signalled by a blast on the ship's siren at noon. On board troopers the men passed the time with protracted sessions of the old army game of 'housey-housey' or organized illicit gambling parties of 'crown and anchor'.

26

At Port Said the gully-gully man came on board and conjured with day-old chicks. His gully-gully patter included addressing all male members of his audience as 'Mr Mackenzie' and female members as 'Lily Langtrie', 'Mrs Simpson' or by whatever name was most notorious at the time, falling back occasionally on 'Annie Laurie'.

'Home-side' and 'Suez-side'. 'From the time you reach Suez and throughout your tour until you have repassed it on your return home, *fear the sun*' (from the Hon. Mrs Lyttleton's *How to Pack, How to Dress, How to Keep Well on a Winter Tour of India (for Ladies)* published in 1892). At Port Said lady passengers landed under escort to visit Simon Artz and to purchase extravagantly outdated sun-hats, which friends or relatives in India would replace with more practical 'Bombay bowlers' or 'double *terais*'.

Undress was acceptable on deck before breakfast. This was an extension of a practice from the days before electric fans and ship's ventilation systems, when male passengers were allowed to bring their bedding up on deck during the Hot Weather months. As more and more women began to come out the custom was modified to allow ladies to occupy the decks on one side of the ship while gentlemen remained on the other. All mattresses and bedding had to be removed before the ship's lascars sluiced down the decks in the morning.

Early morning exercises
Keeping up his polo
SS Egypt

28

King Amanullah of Afghanistan lands at the Gateway of India, 1927. Passenger liners docked at Bombay's Ballard Pier where shipping agents came aboard and, for favours related to the amount of duty saved, eased their clients through customs and onto the waiting trains. Travellers proceeding north caught the Frontier Mail, those going east towards Calcutta – a distance of 1421 miles – the Imperial Indian Mail (first-class passengers only but with coupés for servants).

ON ARRIVAL IN THE EAST

ON disembarking at Bombay, Members will find the Society's representative there to meet them, ready to make arrangements for travellers and do everything possible to assist with their baggage, railway tickets, and accommodation. This is the first service that the Society is able to render its members on arrival in India, but one that is of immense assistance to all new-comers to the East.

The Indian railway station: a bedlam of noise and movement that reached its peak as trains drew in or prepared to pull out. Its most distinctive features were the vendors – selling tea, water, fruit, toys, peanuts and betel nuts, each with their own identifying cry – and the railway coolies, in red shirts and brass arm-bands, who fought for the privilege of carrying huge loads for 2 annas per lift (rather less than a penny). An indispensable part of the traveller's luggage was the *bistra* or bedding roll (shown in the left foreground of the sketch).

'And truly the Grand Trunk Road is a wonderful spectacle. It runs straight, bearing without crowding India's traffic for fifteen hundred miles – such a river of life as nowhere else exists in the world.' The old Grand Trunk Road of Kipling's *Kim*, here photographed with ammunition wagons passing in 1885. While the British pushed on with the railways they were less concerned with modernizing the primitive road systems inherited from the Moguls.

Wheeler's bookstalls were to be found at every major railway station in India. In 1888 six volumes of short stories by an unknown twenty-three-year-old journalist on the *Pioneer* newspaper were issued in a cheap railway library paperback edition, creating the first Rudyard Kipling boom. The covers of these early – and now extremely rare – editions were designed by Rudyard's father, Lockwood Kipling.

Interior of a first-class four-berth compartment, with bathroom attached. Although railway journeys frequently took three or four days, first- and second-class passengers travelled in remarkable comfort, due to the extremely broad gauge of the rolling stock (5'6") and the absence of corridors.

Orders for meals (brought into one's carriage) or for ice-blocks in the Hot Weather (placed in the centre of the compartment in tin trays) could be telegraphed ahead 'up the line'. Only on a few expresses were there dining-cars, which travellers entered at one station and left at the next.

THE PHANTOM 'RICKSHAW & other EERIE TALES by Rudyard Kipling

A. H. Wheeler & Co's Indian Railway Library No. 5 || One Rupee || No. 5

Officers of the 23rd Pioneers camped in the hills, c. 1870, photographed
by Samuel Bourne. Bourne was the greatest photographer of the period and
although he was only in India for a short time his photographs
continued to be used as studies for many years.
The firm of Bourne and Shepherd, based in Calcutta, acquired such status
that no investiture or local durbar was complete without its Bourne and
Shepherd photographer.

2

Anglo-India: The People and the Land

A HOUSE IN THE PUNJAB.

The arrival of the British brought unity to a land which, because of its enormous range of human types, geography and climate, had up till then seemed more like a continent than a country.

Unlike earlier waves of invaders, who had broken through the great mountain barriers of the north, the British came by way of the sea-gates of India, landing as traders and moving inland only by degrees, as though drawn in by the vacuum created by the collapse of the Mogul empire.

They saw India rather as Caesar had seen Gaul, as a land made up of three principal parts. In the south there was the great peninsular plateau peopled by ancient Dravidians and fringed along the coasts of Malabar and Coromandel by European enclaves - Portuguese Goa, French Pondicherry, British Madras. In the centre there was the belt of maximum European penetration, along the courses of the great rivers, across land so flat that it rose barely seven hundred feet in the thousand miles between Calcutta and Delhi. Finally, there was a belt of what Lord Curzon called 'buffer states'; the thinly populated Himalayan ranges to the north, extending downwards on their western and eastern flanks into the great deserts of Baluchistan and the tropical rain-forests of Burma.

'Famine is the horizon of the Indian villager,' wrote Aberigh-Mackay. 'Insufficient food is his foreground.' Droughts, floods and cyclones were all part of the Indian landscape and there was little the British or anybody else could do about it. They built railways, bridges, dams, barrages, canals and great irrigation schemes, introduced tea to Assam and jute to Bengal but, in purely physical terms, their impact remained curiously muted. In the three Presidency cities – Madras, Calcutta and Bombay – and in such provincial capitals as Allahabad and Lahore, the British way of life was impressively represented by grandiose law courts and railway stations, neat civil lines and cantonments. But away from these centres, in what the Anglo-Indians like to call 'up-country' or the *mofussil*, the Indian landscape remained largely unaffected.

Away from the railways transport varied to suit the local geography. The camel excelled in the deserts of Sind and Rajasthan and the elephant in the forests of Assam and Burma. In the Hills coolies carried *dandies* or *doolies* and pulled *jampans* (rickshaws), while in the plains bullock-carts and various forms of horse-drawn vehicles – *ekkas* (hackneys), *tongas*, *gharries*, *tum-tums* (tandems) and *fittons* (phaetons) – provided transport in varying degrees of comfort.

Just as the elephant was associated with princely India so the horse, rather than the motor-car, remained identified with Anglo-India. Long after the car had become a standard household item all civil and military officers were still required to pass riding examinations and government officials were still being asked to tour on horseback. Outside the city the car remained a useful but fragile intruder, whereas a stable of Australian 'walers' (from New South Wales) and sturdy 'country-breds' not only provided local transport but also satisfied the lust for exercise so characteristic of the British in India.

Common government, law and language made less of India's social divisions. Education and easier forms of communication – posts, telegraphs and, above all, the railways – speeded up the process. A large Western-educated middle class was built up, typified by the Bengali *babu*, whom the British professed to find servile and unattractive. In contrast to the 'effeminate' Bengali, they preferred the 'manly' races from the north – the Sikhs and Punjabis, the simple cultivators and the so-called 'martial' races that they drew upon to make up the bulk of the Indian Army.

33

The usual up-country bungalow was a model of functional architecture, entirely without frills. It was usually built by Army or Public Works Department engineers with limited means and equally limited imaginations. The style remained virtually the same throughout the period of the Raj, the main variation being found in eastern India where heavier rainfall demanded a sloping – usually thatch – roof.

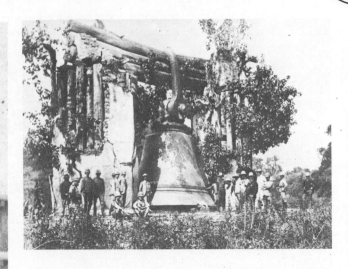

Top right:
The Mengohn temple bell in the forests outside Mandalay, photographed during the annexation of Upper Burma in 1886. Burma lay beyond the natural geography of the Indian sub-continent but eventually became an awkward, unhealthy and unpopular province of the Indian Empire.

Centre:
A Bengal river-steamer on the Upper Brahmaputra, providing the main link between Calcutta and the tea gardens of Assam.

Although life on the plains of northern India centred on the rivers, large-scale navigation was too hazardous and uncertain for them to become major life-lines.

Bottom:
The Sukkur barrage, completed in 1932. The harnessing of the Indus and its tributaries, with the consequent irrigation of large tracts of the Sind desert and the Punjab, was one of the more obvious and lasting achievements of the Raj.

35

Famine in Belgaum, 1876-7. The scourge of starvation was never totally absent from the countryside, where the failure of one rice-crop could easily mean the loss of a million lives. Major famines devastated the land about once in every twenty years but became less catastrophic as the railways spread across the country.

Golden elephant 'four in hand' owned by the Maharajah of Darbhanga. Although some jungle districts did have their official allotment of elephants they were not as much a feature of British India as they were of the native states. One notable exception was Burma where such firms as the Bombay Burmah Trading Company kept 'stables' several hundred strong for work in the teak forests.

Missionaries travelling up-country. The pace of India was essentially that of the bullock-cart outside the cities. The motor-car was no real match for Indian roads, most of which were made of *kunkur* (hard lime), gave off great clouds of dust in the summer and fell to pieces in the Rains.

The effects of the monsoon, Baroda, August 1927, when sixty inches of rainfall were registered in four days; one of the natural hazards faced by the railway officer in his daily work. Other classic situations involved wild elephants on the line, station-masters besieged by tigers and awkward maharajahs who would allow no beef to be eaten on trains that crossed their territory.

Nowhere was the self-confidence of the new rulers better shown than in their public architecture, and few cities better expressed imperial grandeur than Madras, oldest of the three Presidencies and starting-point of the drive into the hinterland that ended in 1857. By the beginning of the nineteenth century the focus had shifted to Calcutta, the 'city of palaces' that became Kipling's 'city of dreadful night'. In the middle of the century Bombay also rose to prominence (much helped by the export of cotton during the American Civil War) and Madras became something of a backwater.

Model of the Hyderabad Residency, in the Begum's garden at Hyderabad, reckoned to be the grandest of the British Residencies in the native states and built by Major James Kirkpatrick, a remarkable eccentric, to give 'an outward appearance of power'.

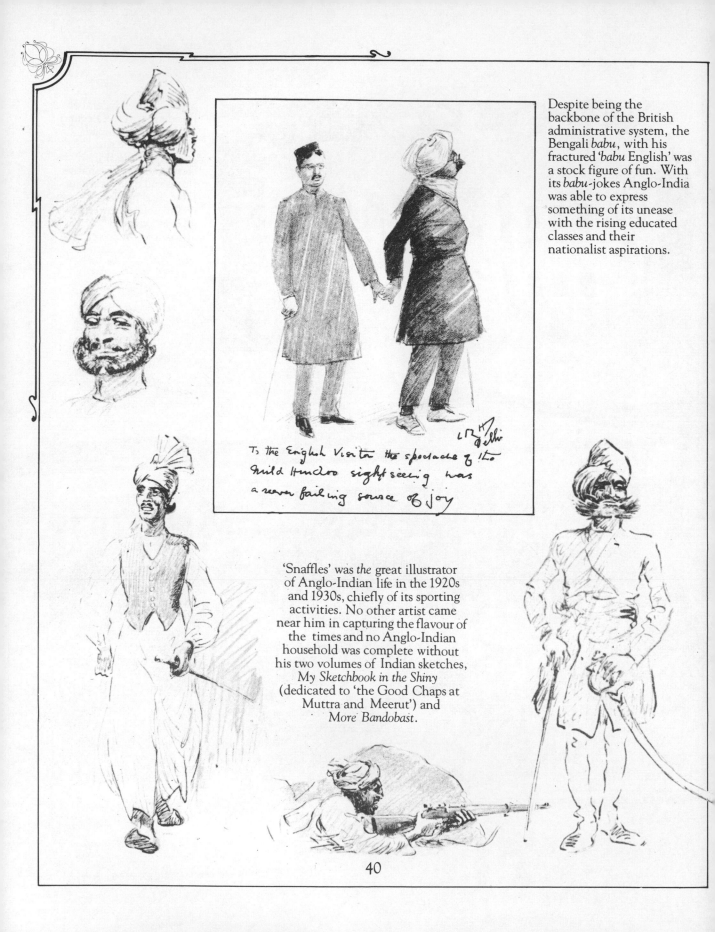

Despite being the backbone of the British administrative system, the Bengali *babu*, with his fractured *'babu* English' was a stock figure of fun. With its *babu*-jokes Anglo-India was able to express something of its unease with the rising educated classes and their nationalist aspirations.

To the English Visitor the spectacle of the mild Hindoo sightseeing was a never failing source of joy

'Snaffles' was *the* great illustrator of Anglo-Indian life in the 1920s and 1930s, chiefly of its sporting activities. No other artist came near him in capturing the flavour of the times and no Anglo-Indian household was complete without his two volumes of Indian sketches, *My Sketchbook in the Shiny* (dedicated to 'the Good Chaps at Muttra and Meerut') and *More Bandobast.*

Twentieth-century English culture, as seen through Indian eyes: an early bioscopic epic.

Bioscope Theatre.

AT MUNICIPAL PARK, CUTTACK.

Electric fitting throughout the Theatre.

A Stupendous presentation of all the latest films from

The Elphinstone Bioscope of Calcutta.

Two shows on every Saturday, Sunday and Wednesday
AT 6-30 AND 9-30 p. m.
and on other days one show at 9-30 p. m.
Entire change of programme every Saturday and Wednesday.

GOLDEN BEETLE.

A thrilling detective Drama in three parts 5,000 feet of real Sensational subjects.

COME & SEE   GOLDEN BEETLE.   See and Enjoy.

THE GOLDEN BEETLE.   THE GOLDEN BEETLE.

Those who miss the golden opportunity of "THE GOLDEN BEETLE"
will pity for ever.

PROGRAMME for Wednesday, Thursday, and Friday.

The 3rd, 4th and 5th October 1917.

1. Oddities of Jim. (comic).
2. Unexpected duty (very comic)

3. Demon of the Rail—A railroad drama.
   The train is just escaped from a collusion.
4. Jim's revenge (comic)

INTERVAL.

5. **The Golden Beetle:**—A thrilling drama of 3 parts, 5000 feet long. Some important scenes of the subject:—George was captured in a temple under the cave of the high mountains, and taking out the blood from his arm writes a massage for help on a piece of his shirt. An eagle while taking away the massage was shot by Murray, who dares to the rescue of George by reading the same message. The fight on horse back and thrilling pursuit. Murray was burried alive in jungle upto his shoulders, and while, being eaten by wild eagles, saved by two Indian hunters.   George was escaped by Murray from the high mountanous caves, by the acrobatic feet of 4 men descending a precipice in human lader fashion, and while going to London their boat was under the mercy of the waves by an accidental storm in the sea. However they landed on a mountain, where they suffered by the amazing adventures of Lions. They reached London by the help of a steamer, and while going home, George was again kidnapped by Golden Beetle clan, was tied, merciless on the railroad. An express train crossing over his body and with many other thrilling and sensational scenes, which makes the audiance to stand thair hairs on end, this story, ends with happy results.

6. GOLDEN BEETLE Part II.   7. GOLDEN BEETLE Part III.   8. Settled at Sea (comic).

GOD SAVE THE KING.

RATES OF ADMISSION.

1st Class Rs. 2|-   2nd Class Re. 1|-   3rd Class Bench Re. 0|8|-   4th Class   Re, 0|4
Special accoomodation and separate entrance for Zanana Ladies at same rates.
A female gate keeper will be in attendance.

S. NARIA—P. P.   3-10-1917   M. A. AZIZ—*Manager.*

Utkal Sahitya Press, Cuttack.

The problem of purdah: British attempts to break down the rigid seclusion of both Moslem and Hindu women met with little success, as this evasive letter to the Collector of Laheria Sarai from a prominent Bengali in his district shows. In his reply the Collector speaks of 'India's opportunity' and calls for the 'exercise of various kinds of courage, not the least of which is moral courage'.

Sept. 10, 1914.

Dear sir,

As my wife doesnot know English, she desires me to write this to you, regarding the Ladies' Conference this evening. My wife is extremely thankful to Mrs. Vernede for graciously extending the invitation to her, but regrets very much that, according to the prevailing custom of the country, no Hindu lady is likely to attend the conference, she is afraid to be the solitary exception to it. Moreover, she will feel herself completely stranded in the midst of strangers, and would, I am afraid, make herself awkward as she never attended a meeting all her

Allahabad purdah-club in the early 1930s: a conscious attempt by the leading women in the district – both Indian and English – to mix more freely with their opposite numbers. Allahabad was unusual in the number of highly sophisticated and 'westernized' Kashmiri Brahmin families that lived there – including the Nehrus.

To Night !   LAHERIA-SARAI.   To Night !!

The Great Herculean Circus Troope

Marvellous Feats of Strength.

SHOWN BY

AN INDIAN LADY.

1 The Breaking of an iron chain.
2 Breaking huge boulders by sledge hammer.
3 Wonderful balancing on the trapeze, on a plank suspended in midair.
4 Other Herculean feats of strength etc. etc.
5 Play on wire.

Over 100 wonderful feats shown by the Troope too numerous to mention.

The spectators are kept spell bound from start to finish and remain speechless in admiration and wonder at some of the performance.

Most of the performers are members of the renowned Lady's family, who shows her wonderful feats that have eclipsed the fame of Ram-moorti.

The nation is shining forth again in the wonderful and daring feats of strength shown by a lady hardly out of her teens.

Her feats of strength testify to the indomitable courage and manliness of a powerful nation now adopting themselves to the exegencies of the times in well directed channels, with the bound of law and order The feats do credit to the fair sex and challenge homage and admiration of all alike. Play will be shown according to the wish of the Proprietor.

TICKETS WILL BE AVAILABLE FROM 7-30 p. m.
PLAY BEGINS AT 8-30 p. m. SHARP.

RATES OF ADMISSION.

Royal Seat	...	...	Rs.	20/-
First Class [reserved]	...	Rs.	2/-
Second Class Chair	...	Rs.	1/-
Third Class Bench	...	As.	/8/-
Gallery	...	...	As.	/4/-

For Pardanasheen Females special arrangement on application.

Come early to abide disappointment if the gallery is filled up ground seat is to be given at the gallery rate.

An unusual example of female emancipation: circus poster, 1917. Not until independence forty years later did Indian women begin to emerge into open society.

43

'An aristocracy of working gentlemen': members of the station
club at Murree in 1877, an exclusive retreat where senior
officials could gather in the evening and exchange working gossip.

3

Formal Introductions: The Social Order of the Raj

In many ways, the social order of the Raj resembled the caste system of the Hindus. At the top, corresponding to the priestly caste of the Brahmins, there were the senior government services: the ICS, the Indian Police, Forest and Medical Services and the lesser Provincial Government services. Then there was the military order, corresponding to the Hindu warrior caste, the Kshatrias, made up of British Army as well as Indian Army Officers. The former judged themselves to be superior, principally because they needed to have a private income to support themselves, while the latter looked-upon themselves as better soldiers, partly because they headed the Sandhurst examination lists.

Next in the social order came the British businessmen, corresponding closely to the low-caste Vaisyas, and subdivided very sharply into commerce and trade. The fourth Hindu caste was that of the Sudras, the outcasts, which as far as Anglo-India was concerned meant the ordinary British soldier and, some way below him, the Eurasian and the domiciled European.

Within this hierarchy everybody knew exactly where they stood. Every rank was set out in order of seniority in an official Warrant or Order of Precedence and the exact position of every single military and civil officer in the country – together with details of his pay – could be found by glancing through the appropriate Civil or Military Lists.

Because so much of its life was bound up with official business, Anglo-India made much of protocol, formality and conformity in dress and de-

PRIVATE.   Monday, 9th March 1936.

THE VICEROY'S HOUSE, NEW DELHI.
—
ARRANGEMENTS.

Date.	A.-D.-Cs. on duty.	Standard Time.	ENGAGEMENTS.
Monday, March 9	Captain Freeman-Thomas.	6·39 a. m.	SUNRISE.
		10·0 a. m.	The Viceroy will see the Hon'ble Law Member.
	Captain Danbeny.	11·0 a. m.	The Viceroy will receive His Exalted Highness the Nizam of Hyderabad.
	Ft.-Lt. Johnson.	11·30 a. m.	The Viceroy will interview Sardar Bahadur Sardar Sir Jawahar Singh.
		12 noon	The Viceroy will see the Secretary, Foreign Department.
			The following will leave The Viceroy's House :—
		...	The Hon'ble Sir Robert, Lady and Miss Reid.
		...	Lieut.-General Sir Ivo and Lady Vesey, Miss Fowke and Captain H. De Pree.
		4·45 p. m.	Their Excellencies will have tea with Their Highnesses the Nawab and Begum Sahiba of Rampur at Maiden's Hotel.
		6·25 p. m.	SUNSET.
		Before dinner	General Sir Kenneth Wigram, the Hon'ble Anne Wigram, and Captain A. Goring will leave The Viceroy's House.
		9·25 p. m.	Their Excellencies will attend an out-of-door performance at the I. D. G. Club of MERRIE ENGLAND in aid of the Diocesan Women's Hostel, Delhi.
		9·30 p. m.	The Viceroy's Band will play for a performance of Merrie England at the I. D. G. Club.
		10·15 p. m.	Major F. Yeats-Brown will arrive (by car) to stay at The Viceroy's House.

The Viceroy or the 'Great Ornamental' was 'the axis of India, the centre round which the Empire rotates'. But he was also, in the words of *Twenty-One Days in India*, 'the centre of a world with which he has no affinity . . . necessarily screened from all knowledge of India'.

portment. The first duty of the newcomer was to call upon the principal members of the station, dressed in his most formal clothes, and leave his card. In due course, his card would be returned, together with an invitation to dinner.

Newcomers were also expected to have themselves put up for election to the station club, the social as well as the sporting centre of the station. Indian membership of such clubs became a highly sensitive issue between the wars, only partly resolved by letting in Indian officers serving in the ICS or in other 'Indianized' services. Yet the exclusiveness practised was not one of race but of kind. These were gentlemen's clubs and those who were not thought to be gentlemen – mostly those in commerce or trade ('counter-jumpers') or the Eurasians – were expected to form their own clubs. Nor was it uncommon for members to be required to resign when they married and to be re-elected only when their wives had been 'vetted'. Ladies were not allowed into the bar. Instead, an area known as the *moorghi khana* (hen house) was set aside for them.

If such outward symbols of convention as the topee and the spine-pad – and indeed such hidden ones as the cholera belt or flannel worn next to the skin – now seem rather ridiculous, it is worth recalling how extreme were the conditions under which the Anglo-Indians lived and worked. Disease, sickness and death were constant companions. Sand-fly fever, malaria, '*dhobie* itch' and dysentry were part of daily life; the threat of cholera, typhoid, smallpox and rabies never far away.

The Collector and his lady, Madras Presidency, c. 1905. 'To the people of India the Collector is the Imperial Government. He watches over their welfare in many facets which reflect our civilization. He establishes schools, dispensaries, gaols, and courts of justice. He levies the rent on their fields, he fixes the tariff, and he nominates every appointment, from that of road-sweeper or constable, to the great blood-sucking officers round the Court and Treasury'. From *Twenty-One Days in India*.

Cartoon by 'Ahmed' in the *Pioneer*, 1938.

" PROVINCIAL SERVICE, I THINK !"

A rival to the talking mongoose has been found in Ferozepore. This is Bhola Nath, a performing bull, which is said to be able to detect members of the I.C.S. at sight.

Seating list for a Government House *burra khana*, Allahabad, 1935. British India's hierarchy followed a strict order of precedence, and hostesses giving a *burra khana* did well to consult their Civil Lists before sitting their guests down to dinner.

Hon. Sir Charles and Lady Kendall
Hon. Mr. Justice Niamat Ullah
Hon. Mr. Justice and Mrs. E. Bennet
Hon. Mr. Justice A. T. Harries
Hon. Mr. Justice U. S. Bajpai
The Rt. Rev. Bishop of Lucknow and Mrs. Saunders
Mr. A. C. Gupta
Mr. and Mrs. T. B. W. Bishop
Pandit Tej Narain Mulla
Mr. and Mrs. R. E. Rutherford
Lieut.-Col. W. A. Montgomery
Mr. P. Biggane
Lieut.-Col. and Mrs. R. S. Weir
Mr. and Mrs. R. T. Shivdasani
Mr. and Mrs. B. G. Prothero Thomas
Major and Mrs. H. L. Watkis
Miss B. Jones
Miss Kendall

_____

HIS EXCELLENCY AND LADY HAIG
Major and Mrs. Brett
Captain Macmullen
Mr. Whitehouse

(33)

Captain Macmullen

Major Watkis	Lieut.-Col. Weir
Lieut.-Col. Montgomery	Mrs. Brett
Miss Jones	Pandit Tej Narain Mulla
Mr. Bishop	Mrs. Shivdasani
Mrs. Weir	Hon. Mr. Justice Bajpai
Hon. Mr. Justice Harries	Mrs. Saunders
Mrs. Bennet	Hon. Sir Charles Kendall
HIS EXCELLENCY	LADY HAIG
Lady Kendall	Hon. Mr. Justice Niamat Ullah
Hon. Mr. Justice Bennet	Mrs. Bishop
Mrs. Rutherford	The Bishop of Lucknow
Mr. Gupta	Mrs. Prothero Thomas
Mrs. Watkis	Mr. Rutherford
Mr. Biggane	Miss Kendall
Mr. Shivdasani	Mr. Prothero Thomas
Major Brett	

Mr. Whitehouse

↑

ENTRANCE

'Officers and Gentlemen', Ahmednagar, 1902. The Indian Army had its own unofficial, but clearly established order of precedence, headed by the Guides and such mounted regiments as Skinner's Horse ('the Yellowboys') or Sam Browne's Cavalry. The Gurkhas generally headed the infantry regiments, followed by the Sikhs and Punjabis. The various ordnance, service and pioneer corps came at the bottom of the list. When the organization of the Indian Army was explained to the new Commander-in-Chief, Lord Kitchener, he replied that, rather than an Indian Army, there seemed to be 'a number of small armies . . . each probably thinking itself superior to the rest'.

Political officers on the Gilgit Mission, 1886. Politicals' were drawn from both the Indian Army and the ICS, some serving as Residents in the native states, some as Agents in the politically sensitive frontier regions. Fear of the 'Russian peril' led to increased British activity along the North-West Frontier, which came to a head with the great frontier uprising of 1897.

Kipling's 'Single Men in Barracks', c. 1890. The notorious remark usually attributed to Lady Curzon, that 'the two ugliest things in India are a water-buffalo and a British soldier', summed up the feeling of the BOR (British Other Ranks) that his presence in India was not appreciated. He usually served four or five of his seven years before the colours in India, in conditions that scarcely changed or improved during the ninety years of the Raj.

Guests are earnestly requested that they should line up on both sides of the hall, preferably Mr. and Mrs. together, otherwise single. After presentation they are requested to go to the Dining table and wait for Their Excellencies till Their Excellencies are seated. It is essential that they should keep their cards ready to announce their names when presented to Their Excellencies.

The wearing of gloves by ladies at Dinner Parties at Belvedere this year will be optional owing to gloves being difficult to obtain as a result of the war.

Indian and Anglo-Indian court etiquette: both Raj and princely India made much of pomp and protocol, in keeping with longstanding Mogul traditions which laid the stress on outward shows of strength and majesty.

PROCEDURE AT THE EUROPEAN DURBAR.

The European Durbar will be held at the Palace at 7-0 P.M. on Wednesday the 17th October 1934.

The Dress to be worn will be as follows :—

FOR CIVIL OFFICERS	... Levee Dress Uniform.
FOR MILITARY OFFICERS ...	Full Dress Uniform or Review Order, Khaki Drill, with medals (for those officers who do not possess Full Dress).
FOR LADIES AND GENTLEMEN NOT ENTITLED TO WEAR UNIFORM.	Evening Dress (full) with decorations.

Officers entitled to wear uniform are not permitted to appear in evening dress.

The route to the Palace will be *via* the Doddakere Tank Road and the Ambavilas Road to the Southern, or Ambavilas, entrance to the Palace.

Ladies and gentlemen are requested to arrive at the Ambavilas entrance not later than 6-45 P.M. Thence they will be conducted to the Main Durbar Hall, where they will await the arrival of His Highness the Maharaja.

After His Highness is seated on the Throne, the ladies and gentlemen will advance in single file, as far as possible in order of precedence. As each lady or gentleman reaches the place at which the Assistant Secretary is stationed, he or she will show the card attached to the invitation and will wait until the name of the lady or gentleman immediately preceding has been announced, when he or she will pass on and hand the card to the Private Secretary, who will announce the name. The lady or gentleman presented will advance to a position opposite to the Throne and bow to His Highness the Maharaja. He or she will then proceed to the seat which will be indicated by the officer in attendance.

It is particularly requested that ladies and gentlemen will maintain silence and will not leave or move their seats during the continuance of the Durbar proceedings.

After an interval, the Hon'ble the Resident will be presented with garland, *attar* and *pan* by the Dewan, and will take his departure. The other guests will then be garlanded.

The guests will then again pass in front of the Throne, bowing to His Highness the Maharaja as before, and will take their departure.

MYSORE,
Dated 3rd October 1934.

Tea planters and indigo planters were looked upon with rather mixed feelings by the rest of the European community. Mostly self-made men, they worked hard and lived hard – and were quite as hard on their labour as themselves. Until the collapse of the indigo trade at the turn of the century, the indigo planter lived the life of a 'farmer prince' and did very much as he pleased. Darjeeling tea garden, 1870s.

Dundee High School old boys' reunion, Peliti's restaurant, Calcutta, 1928. The mercantile community which dominated Calcutta was itself dominated by Scots. The jute industry, in particular, was run almost entirely by Scots 'jute-*wallahs*' recruited from Dundee. Since many of them were manual workers rather than managerial, jute-*wallahs* were regarded as socially inferior by the rest of the mercantile community.

Medical missionaries in camp, central India, *c.* 1905. Until an understanding was reached at the Bangalore Conference of 1908, a good deal of 'poaching' went on between the different mission groups working in India. Among caste Hindus and Moslems there were few conversions. The missionaries had more success with those outside Indian society – the untouchables, aboriginals and hill tribes.

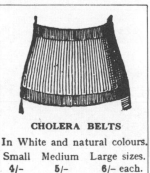

CHOLERA BELTS

In White and natural colours.
Small   Medium   Large sizes.
4/-   5/-   6/- each.

Above left, an Army issue spine-pad intended to protect the spinal column from the effects of the sun and, *above right*, a cholera belt from an Army & Navy catalogue. Although the precise cause of *cholera morbus* (known as 'Corporal Forbes' to British troops), 'the most dreaded of all diseases', was known by 1884, the belief persisted that it was 'an invisible poison, which may be transmitted from adjacent places through the air', and could be brought on by 'immoderate indulgence, viz. eating oysters, unripe fruit and indigestible food'. After a cholera outbreak troops frequently took to 'cholera-dodging', which meant marching up-wind to a 'cholera camp' (often found outside major cantonments).

The Madras Club, *right*, was one of the oldest and grandest in India, and was one of the last to allow Indians to join as full members.
The two great clubs of Calcutta were the United Services Club, which was the oldest in India and did not allow box-*wallahs* as members, and the Bengal Club, which opened its doors only to leading members of the mercantile community and *burra*-sahibs. Calcutta was always very etiquette conscious; even after 1945 office-*wallahs* who stopped by after work for a round of billiards at the comparatively informal Saturday Club were still required to slip out by the back door if they had not donned dinner-jackets by nine o'clock.

Victims of prejudice from both sides: Eurasian station-master and engine-drivers, Vellore, South India, *c.* 1880. 'To the thoroughbred Anglo-Indian, whose blood was distilled through Haileybury for three generations, and whose cousins to the fourth degree are Collectors and Indian Army colonels, the Eurasian, however fair he may be, is a bête noire. Mrs Ellenborough Higgins is always setting or pointing at black blood.' From *Twenty-One Days in India.*

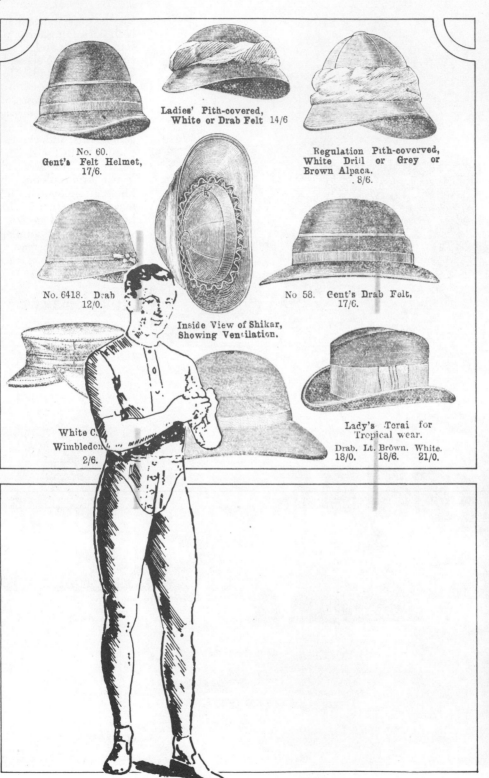

No. 60.
Gent's Felt Helmet,
17/6.

Ladies' Pith-covered,
White or Drab Felt 14/6

Regulation Pith-coverved,
White Drill or Grey or
Brown Alpaca.
8/6.

No. 6418. Drab
12/0.

Inside View of Shikar,
Showing Ventilation.

No 58. Gent's Drab Felt,
17/6.

White C.
Wimbledon
2/6.

Lady's Terai for
Tropical wear.
Drab. Lt. Brown. White.
18/0. 18/6. 21/0.

There were two kinds of topee – the *sola* (pith) helmet made of vegetable fibre, which tended to sag when rained upon, and the heavier cork helmet – both worn in the early days with a *puggaree* (turban) wrapped about them. The most popular up-country topee was the Cawnpore

Tent Club helmet, which remained in fashion for over half a century. During the Cold Weather they were replaced by panamas, straw boaters or 'double *terais*', which were made up of two layers of felt. It was considered very bad form to go out in a topee after sundown.

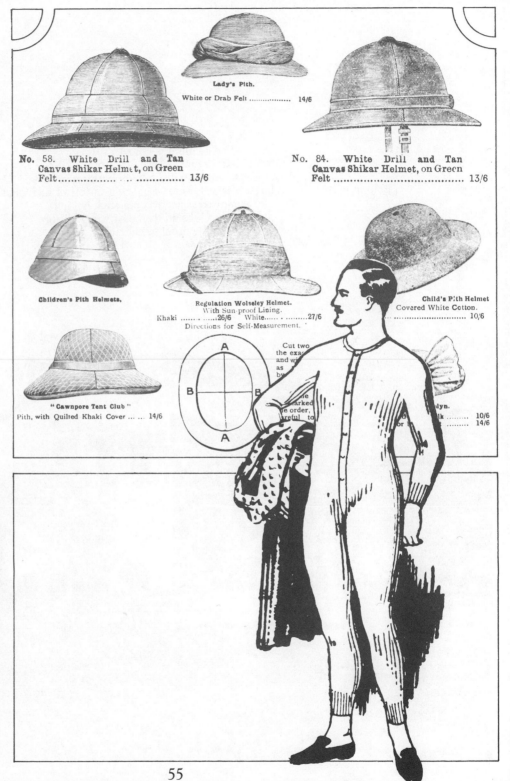

Lady's Pith.

White or Drab Felt 14/6

No. 58. White Drill and Tan Canvas Shikar Helmet, on Green Felt 13/6

No. 84. White Drill and Tan Canvas Shikar Helmet, on Green Felt 13/6

Children's Pith Helmets.

Regulation Wolseley Helmet.
With Sun-proof Lining.
Khaki ....26/6 White...... · 27/6
Directions for Self-Measurement.

Child's Pith Helmet
Covered White Cotton.
.... 10/6

"Cawnpore Tent Club"
Pith, with Quilted Khaki Cover 14/6

Cut two
the exa
and wi
as
b

e
arked
e order,
reful to

lyn.
lk   10/6
or 14/6

The gymkhana club, *c.* 1910:
focal point of most of the off-duty activities
of the station but with the emphasis on sport –
polo in particular. In larger stations there would be a variety of such clubs – 'tent clubs'
for organized *shikar* and pig-sticking, golf
clubs, yacht clubs on the coast – in addition
to the usual social clubs.

4
Up-Country: The Station and the Bungalow

In any fair-sized station the visitor could expect to find a number of self-contained communities, each living within its own well-defined district. The Indian populace lived in the old native quarter (with its own far more subtle forms of segregation) with the railway line and railway station marking the unofficial limits. The Eurasian 'railway community' would be found congregated nearby.

Beyond the railway station there might be an area of no man's land, perhaps a *maidan* (open public ground) partially enclosed by European-style offices and public buildings. From here a broad mall would lead into the civil lines, with carefully laid-out roads, neat, shady verges and very often a 'Company *bagh*' (public garden) complete with bandstand. Nearby would be found the church (C of E), the station club and most of the senior officials' bungalows. Further down the mall there might be the police lines and beyond that again the military cantonment, with its own lines, it garrison church, its bazaars and parade grounds.

The bungalows would be set well back from the road, each within its own compound (enclosed area). In style these buildings changed very little during the time of the Raj, although there were distinct local variations, ranging from the thatched up-country bungalows in the east, where rainfall and flooding was heaviest, to the rather dull-looking buildings of upper India, with their flat roofs and arcaded verandahs.

The interior of the bungalow kept very much to one pattern, with large rooms, high ceilings and plain, whitewashed walls. There was nearly always a wide verandah running round the outside of the house, leading through in the front into the liv-

ing-room, with bedroom suites on either side. The living-room led through into a dining-room and a pantry at the back, again with bedrooms and bathrooms on both sides. The kitchen stood back by itself behind the bungalow, near the servants' quarters.

'It is one of the social follies of Indian life that you must keep three servants to do the work of one,' remarks the anonymous 'Lady' authoress of *Indian Outfits and Establishments*, published in 1882. *The European in India* (1878), lists twenty-seven servants for an establishment of 'tolerably well-to-do people in Calcutta society' and fourteen for the household of a a bachelor. Sixty years later the caste demarcations that made such large households unavoidable had eased considerably. A number of fringe occupations – such as *palkee-wallah* (palanquin bearer), *punkah*-coolie or 'grass-cut' (for the horses) – had either disappeared altogether or were fast disappearing from the scene.

However, the core of the household remained the same. Its key figures were the cook and the head bearer, called in some provinces the *khansamah* or butler. There was also the *khitmutgar* (known as 'khit') who waited at table, the bearer (valet), the *mussalchi* (originally torch-bearer but now scullion), the *mehtar* (sweeper) and the *ayah* (lady's or children's maid). In the 1930s this basic staff of seven would have cost the average employer (the more senior he was the more he had to pay) about two hundred rupees a month, roughly double what it cost to employ twice that number in the 1880s. In the meantime, while salaries had remained more or less pegged, the value of the rupee had declined steadily from 2s to 1s 6d.

57

COLD WEATHER SIGNS.

In preparation for traditional Eastern hospitality, "Not at Home" boxes are being put out.

Cartoon by 'Ahmed' in the *Pioneer*, 1938. The tradition of 'calling' and leaving cards at the start of every Cold Weather was said to have its origins in the days when mortality was so high during the summer months that those who had stayed in the plains and survived called on those newly returned from the hills to show that they were still alive. Newcomers to the station were also expected to leave their cards in boxes provided for the purpose. On these occasions it was considered a breach of etiquette for one party to be seen by the other.

Church parade, Rawalpindi garrison church, 1931, with troops carrying rifles into church – a precaution dating back to the outbreak of the Mutiny at Meerut, which began during morning service on Sunday 10 May, 1857. The traditional Sunday morning turnout at church was often followed by an informal social parade in the Company *bagh*, with a regimental band playing in the bandstand. Until the advent of the motor-car the evening *hawa khana* (literally 'eating the air'), in carriages or on horseback, was another set feature of larger stations.

Cavalry officer with personal servants, 1903. Unmarried officers in the Indian Army lived in the mess and generally had no need of any servants other than a personal bearer and an orderly. The former was nearly always a Mohammedan and usually stayed with his sahib until he married.

Jubblepore 'chummery', 1927: a useful institution found on larger stations by which a number of bachelors – perhaps four or five – could share a large house together, messing together at meals and sharing servants.

59

Verandah furniture, from the Army and Navy Stores catalogue, 1905-1910. The open cane-work prevented sweat from gathering and allowed air to circulate.

The classic verandah chair – the Indian chair – was better known as the 'planter's long-sleever' and often came with 'pockets' for holding drinks.

Up-country bungalow, Vizianagram, Madras, 1889. In the foreground the characteristic flower-pots that substituted for flower-beds.

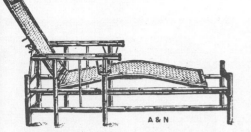
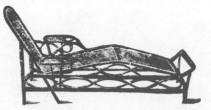
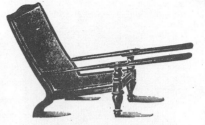

Collector's bungalow, Coimbatore, Madras, 1910: front and verandah. During the Hot Weather the rattan shades would be kept lowered throughout the day. Large pull-*punkahs*, suspended from the ceiling, would be pulled by a rope from outside by a *punkah-wallah*. Breakfast and tea were generally taken on the verandah.

Government House, Mahableshwar, sealed up with *khas-khas tattis*, June 1937. The *khas-khas tatti* was a primitive cooling device – more usually erected across doors and windows – made by pouring water over screens of rough, sweet-smelling *khas-khas* grass. Mahableshwar was the summer retreat for the military station at Poona but was usually abandoned once the Rains came.

Household retinue, probably from the Punjab, 1880s; photographed by Bremner, a professional photographer from Rawalpindi who specialized in military and native scenes. Standing on the verandah are the bearers and *khitmutgars* (in livery), and, on the right, the *dirzee* (seated), the cook, the *ayah* and (with his brush) the sweeper. In the right foreground are the *bheesti* (watercarrier) with his goatskin *mussack* and the *dhobi* (laundryman).

62

THE INDIAN COOKERY BOOK.

A Practical Handbook to the Kitchen in India:

ADAPTED TO THE THREE PRESIDENCIES.

Containing Original and Approved Recipes in every department of Indian Cookery; Recipes for Summer Beverages and Home-made Liqueurs; Medicinal and other Recipes; together with a variety of things worth knowing.

BY A THIRTY-FIVE YEARS' RESIDENT.

The cook, sometimes known as the *bobajee* (more properly, *biwarchi*) was the highest paid member of the household staff. Working with the most primitive equipment – usually no more than a simple mud-brick *chula* – he could produce meals that were little short of culinary miracles, often using Anglo-Indian recipes handed down by word of mouth from his father and grandfather. He also did the daily shopping, taking for himself as much profit – his *dastur* – as his employers would allow him to get away with.

The Indian Housekeeper and Cook

BENGAL.	BOMBAY.	MADRAS.	CEYLON.	BURMAH.
3. *Khitmutgâr*, 10 rs. to 14 rs. Waits at table.	3. *Masauls*, 15 rs. to 20 rs. Waits at table.	3. Mateys, 10 rs. to 15 rs. Waits at table.	3. Boys, 12 rs. to 15 rs. Waits at table.	3. Mateys, 20 rs. Waits at table.
4. *Khansamah*, 10 rs. to 20 rs. Housekeeper and head waiter. Head, as it were, of the commissariat department. A useless servant.	4. None.	4. None.	4. None.	4. None.
5. *Musolchi*, 6 rs. to 10 rs. Scullery man.	5. Cook's Boy, 7 rs. Do.	5. *Tunny ketch*, 6 rs. Cook's help; a woman generally.	5. Kitchen coolie, 5 rs. to 10 rs. Scullery man.	5. Cook's coolie, 12 rs. Kitchen help.
6. *Mehtar*, 6 rs. to 7 rs. Sweeps, underhousemaid.	6. *Humal*, 10 rs. to 15 rs. Does bearers's and superior sweeper's work.	6. *Musolchi*, 8 rs. to 10 rs. As Bombay.	6. House coolie, 10 rs. to 12 rs. Superior sweeper and inferior bearer's work.	6. *Humal*, or house coolie. As Madras, 16 rs.
7. *Bhisti*, 7 rs. Carries water.	7. Waterman, 7 rs. Carries water.	7. Waterman, 6 rs. Carries water.	7. None, except in country.	7. Waterman, 14 rs.
8. *Ayah*, 6 rs. to 10 rs. Lady's maid, nurse.	8. *Ayah*, 12 rs. to 20 rs. Do. do.	8. *Ayah*, 12 rs. to 18 rs. Do. do. Does needlework.	8. *Ayah*, 20 rs. Do. do. Does needlework.	8. *Ayah*, 12 to 18 rs.
9. *Dirzi*, tailor, 10 rs. Not kept in Calcutta.	9. *Dirzi*, 15 rs.	9. *Dirzi*, 10 rs.	9. *Dirzi*. Seldom kept.	9. *Dirzi*. Seldom kept.
10. *Dhobi*, washerman, 10 rs. for two persons, 12 rs. for a family.	10. *Dhobi*, 8 rs. each person.	10. *Dhobi*, 6 rs. each person.	10. *Dhobi*, 5 rs. each person.	10. *Dhobi*, 8 rs. each person.
11. *Syce*, or grooms, 6 rs. to 8 rs. Does groom's work.	11. *Ghora wallahs*, 10 rs. to 15 rs. Do.	11. Horsekeepers, 7 rs. to 10 rs. Do.	11. Horsekeepers, 12 rs. Do.	11. *Syce*, 12 rs. Do.
12. Grasscutters, 5 rs. to 6 rs. Seldom kept.	12. Grasscutters, 6 rs. Seldom kept.	12. Grasscutters, 6 rs. Seldom kept.	12. None kept. Women bring grass.	12. Grass generally bought.
13. Gardener, *Mâlee*, 5 rs. to 30 rs.	13. *Mâlee*, 5 rs. to 30 rs.	13. *Mâlee*, 5 rs. to 6 rs.	13. Gardener, 10 rs. to 12 rs.	13. Seldom kept.

Servants and their wages, from Flora Annie Steel's *The Complete Indian Housekeeper and Cook*, 1905, first published in 1898, and Anglo-India's equivalent of Mrs Beeton's *Everyday Cookery and Housekeeping*. Bachelors did well to consult Major Shadwell's *Economy of the Chummery, Home, Mess and Club*.

REFRIGERATORS
NEW DRY-AIR CABINET REFRIGERATORS

This is a most efficient Cabinet Refrigerator, with the latest improvements. The ice is placed in a wire basket, which is suspended so that the air has free access to it, thus giving the largest possible cooling surface; water from the melting ice cannot enter the refrigerating chamber. The whole of the internal fittings can easily be removed for cleaning. The Refrigerator is constructed of the best materials, and is thoroughly insulated on all sides, lid, door, and bottom.

Before the days of refrigerators ice was Anglo-India's greatest luxury. At first it was landed in Bombay and Calcutta from special American cargo ships and sent up-country by train. In the 1880s ice-machines took over and it could be bought locally and kept in zinc-lined *tundices* (iceboxes).

The "Colonial" Refrigerator.

Possesses a positive cold dry air circulation, and that ensures the provision chamber remaining perfectly pure, sweet and clean.

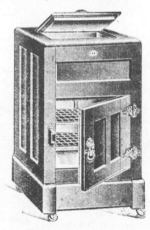

Exterior—polished oak.
Interior—lined with galvanized iron.

No.	Height.	Width.	Depth.	
H 52.	38 by	21 by	13½ in.	.... 59/6
H 53.	39 ,,	23 ,,	15 ,,	.... 78/6
H 54.	41 ,,	26 ,,	17 ,,	...............102/6
H 55.	43 ,,	28 ,,	17½ ,,	...............119/6

Doulton's Household Pattern.
Fig. 63.

Cream Enamelled Stoneware Cases, fitted with Polished White Metal Taps.

Prices :

1 gallon size	13/0
2 ,, ,,	19/0
3 ,, ,,	26/10
4 ,, ,,	35/0
*6 ,, ,,	51/6
*8 ,, ,,	65/9

Fitted with Tubes according to size.

*To order only.

Extra Tubes, 3/3
  ,,   Taps, 2/4

Fig. 72.

Decorated Doulton-Ware Filters.

In the well-known Salt Glazed Stoneware.

They are highly decorative in appearance, but no point of utility is sacrificed.

Fig. 68.
Dining Room Pattern.

2 gallon size	....	43/6
3 ,, ,,	....	61/9

Fig. 72.
Nursery Pattern.

2 gallon size	....	45/9
*2 ,, ,,	....	41/3

*(but in brown stoneware with white figures).

Extra Tubes, 3/3
  ,,   Taps, 2/4

Fig. 68.

Mosquito nets, Army and Navy catalogue, 1905. Although the carrier of malaria had been identified by Ross in Calcutta in 1897 no effective cure was introduced until the introduction of mepacrine in 1942. Quinine was widely used for the treatment of all fevers but caused such side effects as dizziness, deafness and even blindness. Before 1897 malaria or jungle fever was widely regarded, rather like cholera, as 'an invisible vapour floating in the atmosphere . . . most powerful during the hours of night or when a person sleeps'.

Filters, Army and Navy catalogue, 1914. No risks could be taken with the drinking water. In extremis, the addition of alum, potassium permanganate or even a few drops of sulphuric acid was recommended. A more effective system was to place four *chatties* (earthenware vessels) one on top of the other, filling them in turn with gravel, sand and charcoal and allowing boiled water to percolate through to the bottom.

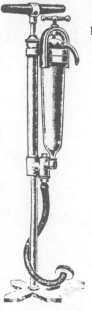

Doulton's "1911" Patent Traveller's Pump Filter.

Each 40/0

British made throughout.

Light in weight and most simple in construction.

The most compact.   Will go in box measuring 12½ by 5 by 4 in. deep.

The joints are unaffected by heat.

Light but strong japanned iron case to take Filter, 4/9.

Extra Tubes, each 3/3

Extra Tubes for all Patterns of Doulton's Filters.

Price .... each 3/3

Doulton's Germ-proof Filters are British made throughout, and are recommended with every confidence.

Recent scientific reports in " The British Medical Journal " and " Journal of Hygiene " showing them to be most effective

'2 ft. 3 in. back to front; seat, 3 ft. long.
Apparatus No. 1a, "Pull-Out" Action.

Receptacles are extra.

PORTABLE EARTH COMMODE.
SUITABLE FOR INDOOR USE.

Throughout the Raj toilet facilities remained simple and primitive. For the evening bath – taken before dressing for dinner – the tub had to be laboriously filled with hot water brought across to the *gussal-khana* (bathroom) by the *bheesti*. Commodes and 'thunderboxes' were serviced by the sweeper or *mehtar*.

L RAVEN HILL

The Indian Bathroom. A sponge would be too convenient a lurking place for scorpions so a tin cups takes its place.

Since liquor was comparatively cheap and thirsts great, drinking habits were controlled by such widespread conventions as not drinking before sunset or after dinner. Fashions in drink changed considerably. In late Victorian times claret and brandy were popular drinks, as was imported East India pale ale. Champagne had a burst of popularity during the Edwardian era. Whisky, pink gin and cocktails, as well as Murree beer, were the drinks of the inter-war period. Spirits were drunk greatly diluted with soda water, known as *billayati-pani* or 'English water', poured out as *pau-pegs* (quarter tots), *chota pegs* (a two fingers' measure) or *burra pegs* (three fingers').

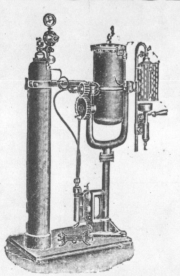

ICS dinner menu, Poona, 1904; a light-hearted interpretation of the duties of the Indian civil servant, chief of which was the settlement of land revenue (as Collector) and the maintenance of law (as District Magistrate). Byculla soufflé (listed on the menu) was said to have originated, like 'egg à la Byculla', from the Byculla Yacht Club at Bombay. Indian cooks were renowned for their soufflés and light pastry.

5

The Sahib: Duty and Red Tape

Recruits to the Indian Civil Service – covenanted officers – entered into a formal covenant between themselves and the Secretary of State for India. Other services had less formal agreements or contracts binding them to equally one-sided terms of service. Officers were liable to dismissal without notice if, for instance, they failed to pass the prescribed linguistic tests.

The Raj made much of its heroes. Chief among them were the legendary figures whose success had come from their capacity to identify with those whom they subdued, men like 'Nikkal Seyn' (John Nicholson), Charles 'Peccavi' Napier and 'Thugee' Sleeman. There were also the stock military heroes who distinguished themselves either in the Mutiny or in the incessant little wars along the Frontier. More significantly, there were Anglo-India's characters, the 'Smith of Asia' and the 'Thompson of Thompsonpore' types and the men on whom Kipling based his 'Gisborne of the Woods and Forests', 'Strickland Sahib' (of the Police), 'Findlayson' (*The Bridge-Builder*) and 'Bobby Wicks' (*Only a Subaltern*), men who, in the familiar aphorism of the time, 'cause two blades of grass to grow where only one grew before.' These were men with a *shauq* (obsessive interest), characters whose eccentricity or strength of personality freed them from the conventions observed by others. Such refreshing exceptions to the rule were greatly admired.

Emphasis on character and personal authority went a long way towards humanizing British rule in India. Whatever line of work he was in, the sahib was expected to play an active role, participating in local work on every level. He was also expected to be accessible to visitors and petitioners and was encouraged with generous travel allowances to go out and see things for himself.

The tour was one of the great institutions of the Raj. It was an opportunity to escape from the drudgery and red tape of the *daftur* (office) and make the most of the Indian Cold Weather. Nearly every branch of government or business managed to tour in one form or another. Collectors and District Officers made their tours across the countryside something of a progress, going out with horses and tents for perhaps two or three weeks at a time, inspecting, administering, enquiring, meeting local officials and dignitaries and generally showing the flag as they went, camping at a new site every night or moving from inspection bungalow to inspection bungalow. Other civil officers toured in much the same way, if rather less elaborately; army officers took their local leaves in the country areas from which their regiment drew its recruits, being received as honoured guests as they went from village to village; railway officers toured in their private carriages, which they could attach to passing trains at will; jute-*wallahs* went deep into the *mofussil* in country-boats and dug-outs to buy their jute; jungle-*wallahs* in the Forest Service and the Survey of India spent more nights out under canvas or in remote inspection huts than they did in their own bungalows.

This was India seen and felt at its best: a perfect climate and relaxed, friendly surroundings close to simple country people. It was the time when Anglo-India felt most at home, knowing that its work was being done.

George Roos-Keppel, Peshawar, *c*. 1904: one of a legendary company of frontiersmen who 'trod daily on the brink of eternity'. Roos-Keppel, Francis Younghusband, Sandeman, the Durands and 'Warburton of the Frontier' were all political agents who combined political guile with a chameleon-like ability to mix with warring tribesmen on the North-West Frontier.

'Bobs Bahadur' and staff, *c*. 1893. Field Marshal Lord Roberts of Kandahar was Commander-in-Chief in India from 1885-93. He was born in Cawnpore, won his VC in the Mutiny and made his name with his famous march on Kandahar. He was immensely popular with both the British and Indian armies. Lady Roberts was said to have been responsible for the closure of army brothels in India.

Andrew Yule was one of half-a-dozen Scots who took advantage of the vacuum created by the break-up of the East India Company to set up a complex structure of managing agency houses that dominated Calcutta by the turn of the century. Managing agencies looked after the local affairs of lesser companies for a percentage of their profits.

Well-salted Anglo-Indians were known as *koi-hais* or *qui-hais*, from the phrase used when calling for servants, said to be the first Hindustani word learnt by newcomers to India.

Andrew Yule.

1889.

3 mango fruits,
24 Nagpur Oranges,
1 pine-apple,
Two phials of excellent hair-oil (a specific for
weakness of brain due to hard mental work &c. &c.)

To

A. H. Verméde, Esq., I.C.S.,
and
Mrs. Verméde,

With the best regards of the Headmaster, Purnea
Zillah Khool, Ramdas Bhattacharyya
8.3.11.

Note accompanying a dolly or presentation tray of gifts to a Collector, 1911. The Mogul custom of *nazrat* (the giving of gifts) was perfectly acceptable in the days of John Company but regarded thereafter as 'bribery and corruption' and combatted with fierce Victorian zeal. For their protection government officers were subject to the *phal-phul* rule, which allowed them to accept only gifts of fruit and flowers.

The North-East Frontier was the 'forgotten frontier' but had its share of military excitements. Surgeon-Captain Newland's photograph of a political officer parleying with hostile tribesmen was taken during a punitive expedition into the Chin Hills, between Assam and Burma, in 1891.

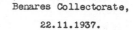

Benares Collectorate,
22.11.1937.

Respected Sir,

We the subordinate officials of Collectorate are highly desirous to pay our respects to your self in connection with the wedding ceremonies and welcome Lady Vernede.

I therefore request you kindly to fix a time which may suit Lady Vernede best and per...us to come to your bungalow to offer our felicitati... welcome on any time tomorrow.

I ...st will mee... ...ent.

I a...

...liently,

Flattery took many forms and was a daily hazard to be faced and ignored by government officials. Petitioners usually prefaced their requests with such phrases as '*Ap ma-bap kai khudawand*' (Lord, you are my father and mother).

73

The Raj at work. *Below left*: Officers of the Public Works Department road surveying beside a government *dak* bungalow (rest house and staging-post), South India, *c.* 1880; *centre*: Railway officers on inspection trollies, Bengal, *c.* 1900; *far right*: Officers of the Survey of India encamped on the Russo-Chinese border, 1912, completing the survey begun by James Rennell in 1764.

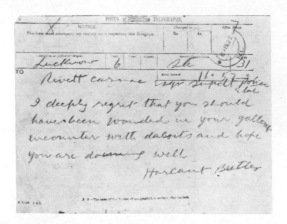

John Rivett-Carnac, Superintendent of Police in Etah, encountered *dacoits* (bandits) while touring in 1921. Armed with a brace of revolvers and clad only in his pyjamas, he charged a large body of *dacoits* attacking a house. After a fierce exchange of fire, in which both he and the leader of the *dacoits* were wounded, he succeeded in putting them to flight.

The office-*wallah*, Calcutta 1937, with his desk littered with paper-weights, which were always necessary wherever there were electric or pull-*punkahs*. Despite the emphasis on outdoor life, the greater part of the day's work was spent in offices, which, in the Hot Weather, became like ovens. In Calcutta, where heat and humidity reached appalling levels in the summer months, work began and finished earlier but went on as normal. Unlike the government services, who removed themselves *en masse* to Darjeeling, most of the business community stuck it out in the plains.

Bottom left: the Western Himalayan ranges, photographed during a surveying expedition in 1912. Forming a majestic background to the plains of northern India, they were seen by the British as a refuge and retreat from the heat of the Indian summer.

Missionaries at work: lady missionary visiting a patient, Bengal, *c.* 1910. The greatest obstacle facing medical missionaries was local superstition and prejudice, particularly in such matters as childbirth and infant care.

CAMP EQUIPMENT
ARTICLES FOR MANŒUVRES AND EXPEDITIONARY USES.

Improved Charpoy Bedstead.
(Registered design, 465534 and 465535.)

This has been designed by the Society with a view to supplying a rigid bedstead, free from hinges or bolts. Size, open 6 ft. 6 in. by 2 ft. 4 in.; closed, 38 in. by 8½ by 7½. Weight about 25 lbs. Ash frame, with Improved Sacking (Reg. design 542,655) 115/9
Mosquito Rods...............................extra 33/0
Green Bag, to hold bed and Rods 7/6

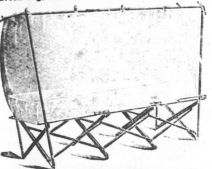

The Improved Compactum Bed, with patent hook joint, and fitted with the Society's mosquito rods and net.
Bedstead, size 2 ft. 4 in. by 6 ft. 4 in.... 74/0
Rods, Wood .... 20/0 and 31/6
Mosquito Net.................................... 50/9

The "Compactum" Camp Bed.

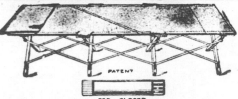

PATENT

BED CLOSED

Size 2 ft 4 in. by 6 ft. 4 in., weight about 20 lb.
Green rot-proof canvas sacking 70/0
Rough canvas Case to carry the "Compactum" Beds 6/9

The Improved X "Compactum" Bed.

This has a greatly superior fitting at the side, which obviates the wear experienced with the old style; size, 2 ft. 4 in. by 6 ft. 4 in.; weight 22 lbs., in green rot-proof canvas.................................. 74/0

Touring in the Cold Weather, South India, *c.* 1890: a government officer breakfasts on the road, complete with dining-table and washstand. The breakfast things would have been sent on ahead at dawn in the covered wagon. The rest of the camping equipment would probably be following on behind and at some point in the day, perhaps over *tiffin* (light lunch) or while he was halted on some local business, would overtake the traveller and be set up at the next camp site.

Camp Bedstead.

The Victoria Camp Bedstead, each 52/0

BATHS.

Canvas Baths, round, in green case 27/0

Note.—Canvas baths are for outdoor use only: a slight leakage is inevitable.

No. B60.

No. B60. Indiarubber Bath, in sponge bag.

No.	B1,	size 27 in.	....	26/0
"	B2	" 30 "	....	27/6
"	B3	" 34 "	....	30/0
"	B4	" 38 "	....	35/3

The "X" Combination Bath and Washstand.
(Green canvas.)

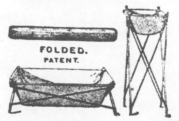

FOLDED.
PATENT.

Complete 55/0
Frame and Basin only 16/0
Frame and Bath and Bag only 49/0
The "X" Bath Frame, with rubber bath fitted, and green canvas bag (no washstand)........................... 32/0

Basins.

Canvas Basin 8/0
Enamelled Iron Basin, 16 in. 7/0
Do., Brass polished, 16 in.................... 20/9
Do., Aluminium, 16 in. 12/9

Covers for Enamelled Iron Basins when travelling.

No. B65a. In leather, 16 in....................... 25/5
In mail canvas, 16 in. 16/6
In green canvas 14/0

Touring was always done in some style since it very often occupied the greater part of the Cold Weather months. In the Punjab, where the nights could be extremely cold, carpets and stoves were regular items of camping equipment. Army and Navy catalogue, 1923-4.

77

Address of welcome printed on silk, presented to the Governor of the Central Provinces during his Cold Weather tour of 1928-9 by the Municipal Committee of Bilaspur, including a request for better roads and drainage schemes. A familiar sign during these progresses was the floral arch with the word WELLCOME (sic) written across it.

All newcomers to the civil and military services were required to sit down and learn the local language, chiefly Urdu or Hindustani, using a *munshi* or scholar. The passing of language exams was rewarded by a pay increase, failure by non-promotion or even dismissal. For many years the set book for Higher Standard Urdu was *From Sepoy to Subedar*, supposedly Sepoy Sita Rama Pandey's account of his thirty years' service with the Bengal Army. The illustration is from Aliph Cheem's *Lays of Ind*.

[Form No. 12.

This is to Certify that *Lieut R. L. Barton*

has passed in Urdu according to the Higher Standard agreeab'y to the provisions of Clause 55, Army Circulars, India, 1895, before the Civil and Military Examination Committee assembled at Bombay on the 4 ... 5 instant.

President of the Civil and Military Examination Committee.

Bombay,
5 September, 1897.

[S 348—200-7-96]

Local justice: the great virtue of the tour was that it allowed local problems and disputes – over boundaries, land taxes or irrigation channels – to be settled on the spot. However, in this instance the malefactor is a Congress 'agitator', appearing before the sub-divisional magistrate after being captured in a police raid on an illegal political meeting (Agra District, December 1930).

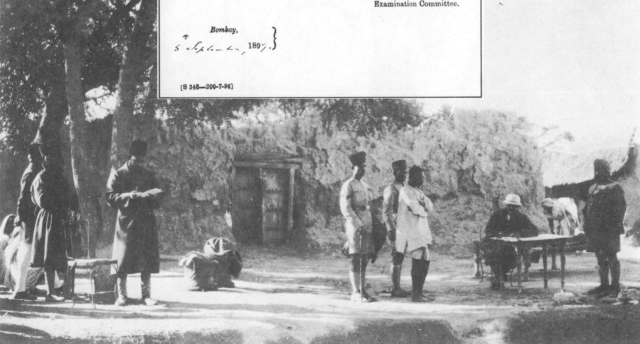

Burra mems at the races, c. 1905. The three leading ladies of the District were the wife of the Collector, the wife of the Superintendent of Police and (if there was a regiment stationed there) the Colonel's Lady. Although the senior lady was indisputably the Collector's wife a considerable degree of rivalry frequently existed between these three leading ladies.

The Memsahib: The Englishwoman in India

'An Anglo-Indian girl's domestic duties are practically nil,' wrote Maud Diver in that famous defence of her 'exiled sisters', *The Englishwoman in India*. 'All things conspire to develop the emotional, pleasure-loving side of her nature . . . that curious slackness – mental and moral – of which the Anglo-Indian woman stands accused.' Maud Diver blamed both custom – 'that insidious tendency to fatalism which lurks in the very air they breathe' – and surroundings, which caused 'an astonishingly rapid waste of nerve tissue, due to the climate and the artificial shifting about life that she leads.'

The memsahib was expected to make a home out of a rented building that she would probably be required to vacate within a year, use furniture and rugs that were hired or made by convicts at the local jail, make something of a garden that annually turned to dust, employ servants who stuck rigidly to the narrowest of demarcation lines, bring up children and nurse them through every possible kind of sickness, knowing that within a few years they would be taken from her.

The only answer, according to Flora Annie Steel, that remarkable lady Inspector of Schools in the Punjab, was to 'make a hold'. Her *Complete Indian Housekeeper and Cook* not only laid out precise guidelines for the memsahib to follow, from how many dusters to give the bearer to treating the bite of a mad dog ('cut with a lancet or penknife to the very bottom of the wound, and again across, so as to let it gape and bleed. Then cauterise remorselessly with nitrate of silver, or carbolic acid, or actual hot iron') but also told her, in brisk, no-nonsense terms, how to make the best of her role in India: 'A woman who wishes to live up to the climate must dress down to it'

. . . 'make the sun your friend' . . . 'don't give in to it (the hot weather) and it will give in to you' . . . 'a languid stroll from your drawing-room to your carriage and back again is *not* sufficient to keep your organism going' . . . 'what remains therefore but race prejudice to account for the fatuity of fearing lest the milk of a native woman (for breast-feeding) should contaminate an English child's character?' Regrettably, the single most useful piece of advice in the book – that the memsahib should learn Hindustani – was the one most frequently ignored.

This was the second stage in the evolution of the memsahib, from the defensive, rather useless minor partner to the active, even aggressive, 'house-mother'. The last stage only became general after the Great War, when memsahibs came down off their pedestals and took it upon themselves to move into Indian society, taking more active roles in the welfare of their household staff or the men under their husband's command, giving purdah parties for their Indian opposite numbers, even taking up nursing, scouting or other forms of voluntary work.

The children led an altogether less complicated existence. While the parents may have bewailed the 'insidious and evil examples and teachings of the native servants', from the point of view of the *chota* sahibs and missy *babas* themselves, childhood in India was nearly always a supremely happy period in their lives. Their *ayahs* (nurses) and servants, with their apparent 'propensity to worship at the shrine of the baba-*log* (baby-people)' may indeed have spoiled them and taught them un-sahiblike ways and tongues but in doing so they gave them an affection for India and Indians that no amount of separation and schooling abroad could ever eradicate.

'Half the cases of neuraesthenia and anaemia among the English ladies, and their general inability to stand the hot weather, arises from the fact that they live virtually in the dark,' wrote Flora Annie Steel. But there were always numerous exceptions to the rule and plenty of *mems* who shared the outdoor pursuits of their husbands. Lady *shikari* (hunter) with her bag, *c*. 1910.

Marked differences in age between bride and bridegroom characterized many Victorian marriages in India. Low starting salaries, poor living conditions and disapproval – both official and unofficial – of early marriage meant that few sahibs married before their late twenties. From the memsahibs' point of view the senior civil servant – said to be worth 'a thousand pounds a year, dead or alive' – was a very eligible prospect.

The Indian *chit* (note) system of signing rather than paying for goods, which went hand-in-hand with virtually unlimited credit for the sahib *logh* (Europeans), made it all too easy to live beyond one's means. Indian pronunciation explains the unusual spelling in the tailor's bill – 'dras' for 'drawers', 'bilvet' for 'velvet', 'escate' for 'skirt'. Airtight trunks and hat-boxes helped to keep down the mildew that damaged clothes and shoes in the Rains.

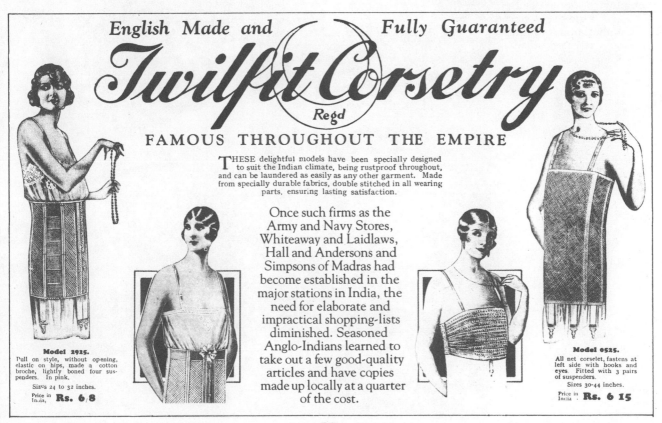

Tea on the lawn, Hosur, Madras, 1905; strictly a Cold Weather phenomenon. The brass *chaprass* (badges) worn by the servants marks them out as government office servants. It was usual for servants to wear the 'colours' of their employers' services in the form of coloured cummerbunds or sashes in their turbans.

84

Above: India was 'the land of the open door' and its chief form of hospitality was dinner, usually taken late (nine o'clock and later in the Hot Weather) and always over-burdened with European hors d'oeuvres, meat dishes, entrées, puddings and savouries.

Below: before the arrival of the airmail service in the late 30s it took six to eight weeks to get a reply to a letter. Despite the time-lag Anglo-India relied heavily on the weekly arrival of the home mail and the English papers, bound into special weekly editions.

The memsahib had plenty of leisure time to devote to such pastimes as painting or reading – and a wealth of Anglo-Indian literature to draw upon at the Club's library. If she disliked satire she could always turn to the romances of such forgotten novelists as Mrs Croker and Mrs Cotes, as well as to that formidable literary duo, Maud Diver and Flora Annie Steel. The latter was not only the joint authoress of *The Complete Indian Housekeeper* but also produced what was often said to be Anglo-India's finest work of fiction, *The Potter's Thumb*. Great efforts were made to make Indian gardens more homely and more English which required the endless watering of wide lawns of coarse *dhoab* grass and careful nurturing of seedlings. Cannas, summer chrysanthemums and marigolds flourished; more sensitive plants withered away with the Hot Weather.

THACKER, SPINK & CO.

BOOKS FOR PRESENTATION.

A NEW EDITION OF A FAMOUS ANGLO-INDIAN CLASSIC.

CURRY & RICE

(ON FORTY PLATES);

OR

THE INGREDIENTS OF SOCIAL LIFE

AT

"OUR" STATION IN INDIA.

BY

Capt. GEO. F. ATKINSON.

Royal 8vo, cloth gilt. Price, Rs. 18-6.

The first Edition of this now very scarce book was published in 1858; the present Edition has been reproduced from the original water color sketches of the artist, especially lent for the purpose, the whole book being as regards letterpress, binding and finish as nearly an exact copy of the original work as it is possible to make it.

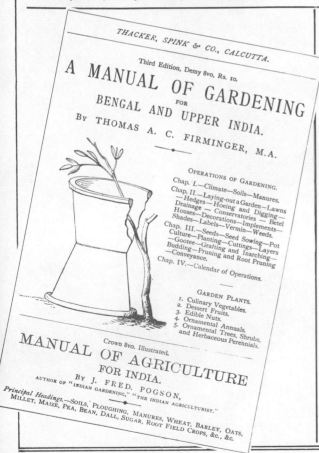

THACKER, SPINK & CO., CALCUTTA.

Third Edition, Demy 8vo, Rs. 10.

A MANUAL OF GARDENING

FOR

BENGAL AND UPPER INDIA.

By THOMAS A. C. FIRMINGER, M.A.

OPERATIONS OF GARDENING.

Chap. I.—Climate—Soils—Manures.
Chap. II.—Laying-out a Garden—Lawns—Hedges—Hoeing and Digging—Drainage—Conservatories—Betel Houses—Decorations—Implements—Shades—Labels—Vermin—Weeds.
Chap. III.—Seeds—Seed Sowing—Pot Culture—Planting—Cuttings—Layers—Gootee—Grafting and Inarching—Budding—Pruning and Root Pruning—Conveyance.
Chap. IV.—Calendar of Operations.

GARDEN PLANTS.
1. Culinary Vegetables.
2. Dessert Fruits.
3. Edible Nuts.
4. Ornamental Annuals.
5. Ornamental Trees, Shrubs, and Herbaceous Perennials.

Crown 8vo. Illustrated.

MANUAL OF AGRICULTURE FOR INDIA.

By J. FRED. POGSON,

AUTHOR OF "INDIAN GARDENING," "THE INDIAN AGRICULTURIST."

Principal Headings.—SOILS, PLOUGHING, MANURES, WHEAT, BARLEY, OATS, MILLET, MAIZE, PEA, BEAN, DALL, SUGAR, ROOT FIELD CROPS, &c., &c.

Eighth Edition. Crown 8vo, cloth. Rs. 4-8.
Handsomely bound in smooth velvet calf, yapp edges, Suitable for Presentation Rs. 7-8.

BEHIND THE BUNGALOW.

By EHA.
With Fifty-three Illustrations by E. C. MACRAE.

"A Little Islope."

Second Edition. Crown 8vo, cloth. Rs. 4-8.
Handsomely bound in smooth velvet calf, yapp edges, Suitable for Presentation. Rs. 7-8.

A NATURALIST ON THE PROWL.

By EHA.
With Eighty Illustrations by R. A. STERNDALE, F.R.G.S., F.Z.S.

Seventh Edition. Crown 8vo, cloth. Rs. 4-8.

Handsomely bound in smooth velvet calf, yapp edges, Suitable for Presentation. Rs. 7-8

THE TRIBES ON MY FRONTIER.

AN INDIAN NATURALIST'S FOREIGN POLICY.

By EHA.
With Fifty Illustrations by F. C. MACRAE.

Children's saddles, Army and Navy catalogue, 1905. Their parents' enthusiasm for riding and daily exercise was so great that it was hardly surprising that even the youngest children were expected to follow suit. An iron ring fixed above the saddle was commonly used to prevent children from falling off.

The children's fancy-dress party was a regular feature of the Anglo-Indian social scene, even if most of them were rather less elaborate than this select children's fancy-dress ball at Viceregal Lodge, Simla, in 1910. It would be unusual to see children older than six or seven at such gatherings, since a whole generation – from seven to seventeen – was always away at school in England.

Childhood in India was a paradise for healthy young *chota* sahibs and missy *babas*, a graveyard for sickly ones; *chota* sahib with *ayah*, head *chaprassi* and dog boy, Bihar, 1906 – 'native servants whose propensity to worship at the shrine of the *baba-log* (children) is unhappily apt to demoralize the small gods and goddesses they serve' (from Maud Diver's *The Englishwoman in India*, 1909).

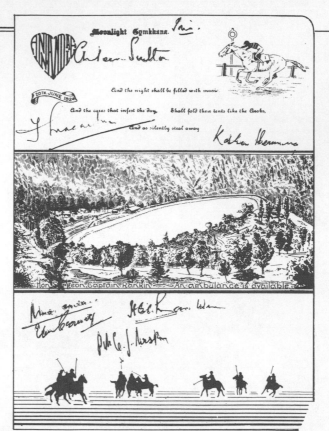

Moonlight Gymkhana. Simi.

And the night shall be filled with music.

And the cares that infest the day,   Shall fold their tents like the Arabs,

And as silently steal away

Hon. Surgeon Captain Rankin.   An ambulance is available.

On the road to Naini Tal, 1904. For women and children the journey to the hills frequently involved travelling in *dandies* (sedan chairs) or *doolies* (palanquins). Senior officials had their own liveried carriers. In Simla only the Viceroy, the Commander-in-Chief and the Governor of the Punjab were allowed motor-cars. Other Europeans walked, rode or went about in rickshaws.

Moonlight gymkhana, held at Annandale race course, Simla 1924, with surgeon and ambulance in attendance. Simla, most glamorous of hill stations and summer capital of both the central and Punjab governments, enjoyed a brief but sophisticated summer season. It was one of the few places in India where the British could relax among their own kind and throw off some of the inhibitions that kept them in check while down in the plains.

'During the hot weather the Briton is not himself. The Indian climate throws its net over him, and struggle as he may he must yield to its embrace.' The traditional means of avoiding the hot weather was to take refuge in the Hills, in the very English atmosphere of the hill stations that the British had built up for themselves along the foothills of the Himalayas – at Murree, Simla, Mussoorie, Naini Tal and Darjeeling – as well as at Ootacamund ('Ooty') in the Nilgiri hills in the south and Shillong in the east. Choonbatty loop; on the way to Darjeeling, built in 1879.

Alligator hunt down the Ganges from Allahabad, *c.* 1900, from
the scrapbook of a District Collector. It required great
accuracy of shooting to kill a *muggur* (broad-nosed alligator).
Skins were sent to the leather tanneries at Cawnpore and
returned as handbags and brief-cases.

7

Off-Duty: The Pursuits of the Raj

'Fortunately the young Englishman requires no incitement whatever towards bodily activity,' writes 'J.E.D.' in his *Notes on an Outfit.* 'The men who look the most fit and who retain best their health and spirits are those who take regular exercise – whether in sport, in games or in their duty.'

Exercise and sport played an enormously important part in the lives of the British in India, making them as fit a group of men and (in later years) women as it was possible to find. The declared reason for this mania for daily exercise was to maintain health in an unhealthy climate, but sport was also a natural device for bringing people together and provided much-needed opportunities for relaxing and letting off steam – an antidote, perhaps, for all the disciplined formalities of the Raj. Almost every large station club had its badminton and squash courts (which gave way to tennis) and latterly, its swimming pool, with swimming becoming increasingly popular in the inter-war years.

The main means of exercise was the horse, which for many people was very much a working animal, taking them out daily on inspection tours or to the more remote places which no motor-car could ever hope to reach. Riding for pure recreation usually took the form of a brisk ride before breakfast and a canter round the *maidan* – perhaps even a scratch *chukka* of polo – in the cool of the evening. Just as the elephant was associated with the native princes so was the horse closely identified with the Raj. Indeed in some quarters – notably in the cavalry regiments – this identification reached a pitch that verged on horse-worship. It was the horse that made possible such genteel entertainment as the gymkhana and the Saturday morning paperchase, as well as polo and such bizarre blood sports as jackal-hunting (complete with imported hounds and masters in pink) and pig-sticking.

India also gave the sportsman with a rod or a gun rare opportunities for *shikar* (shooting and fishing). If he was prepared to make the effort, he could stalk for the rare *Ovis Poli* in the high Karakoram or go after the Indian rhinoceros in the *terai* country bordering on Nepal or Assam. During his first tour he might well go to some lengths to bag a tiger or two, since it was expected of him; but in time the average *shikari* (hunter) settled down to what was the most usual form of Indian *shikar*, slipping out to the nearest patch of scrub or swamp whenever the opportunity showed itself – when he was passing through an up-country district on tour perhaps. On such occasions he generally shot 'for the pot' a jungle fowl, a quail, a partridge or even a black buck, seizing the chance to give a little variety to what was often the most monotonous of diets. If he had any sort of local influence or 'pull', the amateur *shikar* frequently arranged Christmas fishing and shooting in some isolated forest camp, with a few friends to keep him company and a few servants to provide the minimum comforts. This was usually the extent to which most Anglo-Indians indulged in *shikar*, although it was inevitably overshadowed by big game and trophy hunting.

The practice of slaughtering large numbers of tigers or bears and even larger numbers of lesser game animals and birds – wild duck and sand-grouse, in particular – was confined to the Native States. In what were very often the wildest parts of India, quite a number of princes devoted their energies to organizing immensely elaborate camps and shoots, to which they invited Viceroys and Governors and lesser Europeans whenever possible. It would be wrong to think of these as sporting occasions: they were an essential part of the rituals of state, necessary displays of power by princes made largely impotent by the Pax Britannica.

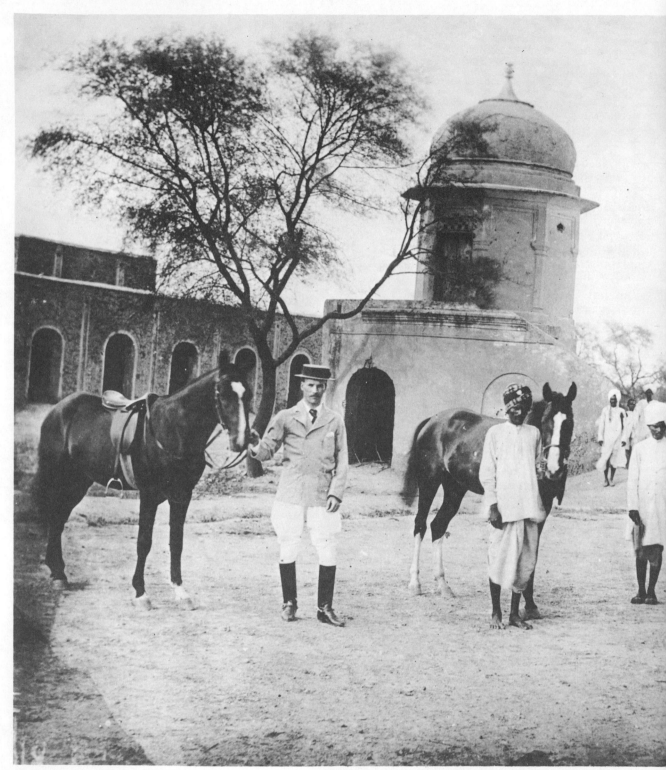

94

The keeping of large stables was encouraged by generous government allowances. In infantry regiments officers could hire 'seven-eighters' from the cavalry for seven-and-a-half rupees a month, while civilians could acquire a polo-playing charger as members of a Light Horse Unit of the Auxiliary Forces (India). Hissar, 1897.

95

The *pagal* or crazy gymkhana was a favourite feature of any sporting 'week' in the Cold Weather. Photograph *c*. 1900. Programme of events from the *Pagal* Gymkhana, Mysore Lancers Parade Ground, 1934.

PROGRAMME OF EVENTS

1. 3·45 P. M.—**Pigsticking.**
   Mounted Individual Event.

2. 4 P. M.—**Tea**—Display of Horsemastership, Mysore Lancers.

3. 4·35 P. M.—**Treasure Hunt.** Among the flower pots. Individual dismounted event.

   Each competitor is alloted a group of inverted flower pots on top of which he or she must walk while looking for an anna piece which is under one flower pot in each group. Touching the ground with foot or hand except with hand to pick up the anna, disqualifies. The first competitor to raise the anna above his head, standing upright on the flower pots wins.

4. 4·15 **Running the Guantlet.**
   Men Mounted.
   Course—Circular course with four or more poles carrying Polo Balls.

   Competitor rides down course in a black coat with a haversack. At each pole he must pick-up the polo ball on the pole and put it in his haversack. At each post outside course, a lady is posted with white-washed tennis balls. The object is to hit competitor with tennis balls as he slows down to pick up Polo ball. After each competitor has completed this course, his coat is examined by Judges for the number of hits on it, and the competitor, with greatest number of Polo balls and the least number of hits, wins.

5. 4·50 P. M.—**Potato Race**—with cars
   Pairs, Lady and Gentleman.

   Gentleman to drive a car along a course within time limit. Lady seated behind to throw a Potato in each of the 4 or 5 buckets placed along the course. The pair with largest number of potatoes in buckets and passed winning post first within the time limit, wins.

6. 5·10 P. M.—**Musical Chair** for ladies.
   A mounted individual event.

7. 5·30 P. M.—**Musical Ride, Mysore Lancers.**
   Note—1. Post entries.
   2. Horses will be provided if required.

THE MADRAS HUNT.

Sir,

Your Committee beg to submit the Annual Report and Accounts for the Season 1901-1902. The latter showing a debit balance of Rs. 1,801-9-8 against which there is still Rs. 1,702-12-0 to be received as shown overleaf.

We shall thus have to commence next season with a small debit balance which is to be regretted, but on the other hand, had not the guarantors responded most nobly to a call of 45 per cent. of the amount guaranteed the situation might have been considerably worse.

The pack, originally consisting of 15 couples purchased for the Hunt in England by Mr. deClermont, to whom the hearty thanks of members are due, arrived rather earlier than usual and most unfortunately came in for a spell of exceptionally hot weather which carried off no less than 7 couple, and had it not been for the kindness of Mr. Yorke in allowing the hounds to be removed to Brodie Castle it is highly probable that the epidemic which prevailed would have carried off the whole pack.

As it would have been impossible to have got along with only 8 couple the Committee decided to replace the deficiencies, and draft consisting of 3½ couples from Bangalore and 3 couple from Poona were purchased, and shortly after we were reinforced by one couple of Australian Hounds drafted from the Sydney Hunt the latter proving quite a success though perhaps a trifle too fast for the others.

Major Logan Home again carried the horn with Mr. Shore and Captains Lygon and Oakes as whips and good sport was shown though towards the latter part of the season drought very much interfered with the mornings' work.

The pack met 22 times and accounted for 18 jacks, and considering the fact that hunting was twice stopped, each time for a period of about 10 days on account of the flooded state of the country, the above figures may be considered satisfactory.

There will be a meeting of Members on Wednesday the 23rd instant at 6-30 p. m. at the Gymkana to make arrangements for hunting the country next season.

H. M. GIBSON,

14th April 1902.   Honorary Secretary.

KENNELS,
ADYAR,
30th November, 1914.

To SUBSCRIBERS,

To THE MADRAS HUNT.

DEAR SIR,

CROP DAMAGE.

I would specially ask all followers of hounds to refrain, as much as possible, from riding over crops.

Where crops are unavoidable, ride single file alongside the bunds. Do not cross the middle of the fields and make lanes all through the paddy.

Most damage is done to paddy in the latter part of the season, when the crop is ready for cutting or is lying cut on the ground, as the ripe seed is then knocked out of the ear and lost.

Never, in any circumstances, ride over garden crops or seed beds; these are always small and easily avoidable.

Remember that even a few annas worth of damage is of material consequence to the small cultivator and that his good will is essential to the sport.

I would ask all regular followers of hounds to assist the Hunt Staff by remonstrating with any thoughtless individual they may see committing this breach of sporting courtesy to the people over whose land we ride.

I am, Dear Sir,

Yours faithfully,

H. N. C. CAMPBELL,

Master.

Meet of Hounds, Ootacamund, c. 1910. Ootacamund was the oldest and – with its rolling open downland – possibly the most English of all the hill stations. It also ran what was probably the finest hunt in India, although the 'PVH' – the Peshawar Vale Hunt – would have been a close second. 'Jacks' (jackals) were said to be quite as sporting as foxes but hounds had to be imported from England and were no match for the Hot Weather.

Watching polo at Dacca,
1904. Polo was first played
by British planters in
eastern Bengal in about
1840 but very soon spread
across India to become
Anglo-India's chief
competitive sport.

Pig-sticking – more
properly the spearing of the
male wild boar with
'hog-spears' – was a
peculiarly Anglo-Indian
sport that flourished in the
plains of upper India. It
was a risky business
demanding cool nerves
and a high degree of
horsemanship. At the
annual Kadir Cup meet
outside Meerut,
hog-hunters competed
against each other in heats
to draw first blood.

Viceroy's bag: Lord Lansdowne shooting as a guest of the Maharajah of Poonch, *c.* 1890. Bags of this order – more usually of tiger – were a feature of princely shoots, where expense was no object and conspicuous destruction everything.

Trophies from six years of *shikar* in the North-West Provinces. A fairly modest bag for that era. The alligator with the salver is a *ghurrial*, a fish-eater, and not considered true sport for *shikaris*.

Number of Guns.	Name.	Place.	Black buck. Number.	Head.	Chinkara. Number.	Head.	Houbara.	Demoiselle Crane.	Duck.	Imperial Sand Grouse.	Sand Grouse.	Partridge.	Snipe.	Total.
					29TH DECEMBER (MORNING).									
1	His Highness	Gajner ...	...	...	...	...	...	...	1	114	...	...	...	115
2	Sir Brian Egerton ...	,, ...	...	...	...	...	...	...	...	44	...	...	...	44
3	Captain Portal	,, ...	...	...	...	...	...	...	...	40	...	...	...	40
4	Sir James Roberts ...	,, ...	...	...	...	..	...	...	...	36	2	...	...	38
5	Colonel Campbell ...	,, ...	...	...	...	...	...	...	...	30	...	...	...	30
6	Colonel Harenc	,, ...	...	...	...	...	...	...	...	28	...	...	...	28
7	His Highness of Alwar ...	,, ...	...	...	...	...	...	...	...	19	...	...	...	19
8	Colonel Waddington ...	,, ...	...	...	...	...	...	...	...	17	5	...	...	22
	Total ...	... ...	...	...	...	...	...	...	1	328	7	...	...	336
	Picked up ...	... ...	...	...	...	...	...	...	1	328	7	..	...	336
1	Junior Prince	Sugansagar...	...	...	...	...	...	...	...	81	7	...	...	88
2	Senior Prince	,, ...	...	...	...	...	...	...	...	52	...	...	...	52
3	Mr. Powell	,, ...	...	...	...	...	...	...	...	37	...	...	...	37
4	Sir Charles MacWatt ...	,, ...	...	...	...	...	...	...	...	29	1	...	...	30
5	Mr. LaTouche	,, ...	...	...	...	...	..	...	...	25	...	...	...	25
6	Major Barbour	,, ...	...	...	...	...	...	...	...	23	2	...	...	25
7	Captain West	,, ...	...	...	...	...	...	...	..	19	...	...	...	19
8	Mr. Cook...	,, ...	...	...	...	...	...	...	...	18	...	...	...	18
9	Mr. Crisp...	,, ...	...	...	...	...	...	...	...	15	...	...	...	15
10	Mr. Jose	,, ...	...	...	...	...	...	...						
11	The Thakur of Rampura...	,, ...	...	...	...	...	...	...						
12	Mr. Rigg...	,, ...	...	...	...	...	....	...						
13	The Thakur of Sarothia ...	,, ...	...	...	...	...	...	...						
14	Mr. Fearfield	,, ...	...	...	...	...	...	...						
15	Mr. Hoefler	,, ...	...	...	...	...	...	...						
16	Captain Powell ...	,, ...	...	...	...	...	...	...						
17	Thakur Bharat Singh ...	,, ...	...	...	...	...	...	...						
18	Mr. Dooris	,, ...	...	...	...	...	...	...						
19	Mr. Walsh	,, ...	...	...	...	...	...	...						
20	The Thakur of Magrasar.	,, ...	...	...	...	...	...	...						
21	Dhabai Ganeshi Lal ...	,, ...	...	...	...	...	...	...						
22	Major Helliwell	,, ...	...	...	...	...	...	...	...	7	...	...	...	7
23	Doctor Knabe	,, ...	...	...	...	...	...	...	...	6	...	...	...	6

During this one morning in a week of concentrated shooting at Bikaner over Christmas, 1931, a total of 787 sand-grouse were shot, with the Maharajah of Bikaner alone (but occupying the best site) accounting for 114.

'A desperate shot – An exciting day's sport', sketched by the *shikari* himself, Lionel Douglas Hearsey, in 1895. In time, the shooting of tigers from the backs of elephants came to be regarded as rather unsporting and best left to princes and visiting VIPs.

101

The Cold Weather camp –
idealized and in reality: the
camp as seen in an
advertisement for a milk
separator, *c*. 1913 and
right, a fishing camp from
the 1880s, with a fine catch
of *mahseer*, the Indian
equivalent of the salmon.

Police sentry and snake,
1930s; the one having
caught the other (a small
cobra) while on sentry
duty outside the Collector's
bungalow. When the
Collector appeared the
sentry stood smartly to
attention with his prey.

A remarkably optimistic
seaside advertisement for
1913, since sea-bathing was
not a fashionable form of
exercise among the British
and both Hindus and
Moslems alike would have
been shocked by the
impropriety of the
costume. Many of the
larger stations and
gymkhana clubs added
swimming-pools to their
private sporting facilities in
the 1920s.

Preparing for a rough shoot
in the *terai* – the scrub
forest bordering the
Himalayan foothills –
Christmas camp, 1936.

A very average infantry regiment: the 2nd Grenadiers (Bombay Native Infantry) and its officers, photographed in 1878. The regiment's greatest battle honour was won at Koregaum in 1818, when five hundred sepoys drove off an army twenty thousand strong. After the Mutiny – when five of its native officers were blown away from guns, three shot, ten hanged and six transported for life – its fortunes declined and officers with ambition preferred to serve with the so-called 'martial' races from the north.

8

The Regiment: Britain's Indian Army

There were always two armies in India – the British Army and the Indian Army, with one British regiment to two Indian in every brigade. After the Mutiny most Indian regiments were reorganized into mixed battalions where one company might be made up of Sikhs, another of Punjabi Moslems, a third of Dogras and a fourth of Rajputs. Only a few 'loyal' regiments – Sikhs, Gurkhas, Marathas – were allowed to continue intact.

As the century proceeded, recruits were increasingly drawn from the northern races, who were for some strange reason deemed to be more 'martial' than those in the south. Orthodox Brahmins (who had formed the bulk of the mutinous Bengal Army) were no longer judged to be fit for army service. An important feature of this new and highly professional army was family connection. Recruits were drawn not only from particular races, but very often from the same clans and villages, with sons following fathers and nephews following their uncles, so that over the years a strong tradition of kinship developed within each regiment. The sense of family was further stressed by the way in which each regiment lived in cantonments as a self-contained community, cutting itself off from the outside world.

Compared with British regiments there were very few British officers in each Indian regiment – in the 1880s no more than seven or eight, with the command of individual companies being left to Viceroy's Commissioned Officers (VCOs) – Indian *subadars*, *jemadars* or *risaldars*. The young officer therefore had rather more responsibility than his contemporaries in the British Army. As a bachelor he made the mess his home and generally enjoyed a very gentlemanly

The backbone of the regiment; Indian VCOs rose through the ranks and exercised a great influence on their men. *Subadar*-Major Naurung Singh, 15th Sikhs, 1917. Not until after the Great War were Indians accepted as fully commissioned King's Officers.

form of existence, with little hard work to do and plenty of leisure time for games (often played with his men) and *shikar*.

Most Britons in uniform in India were soldiers in the British Army. The officers shared the same status and privileges as their counterparts in the Indian Army but the NCOs and men – the British Other Ranks (BORs) – lived a very different kind of life. It was Rudyard Kipling, writing in the 1880s, who first gave Anglo-India some inkling of the harsh lives lived by these 'single men in barracks, most remarkable like you'. Yet of all sections of British society in India it was this class that was least touched by progress over the next sixty years. Right up to the end of the Raj the British common soldier remained uniquely underpaid and underprivileged, kept isolated as a matter of deliberate policy from the rest of India, often spending his entire service there – usually five years and more at a stretch – without so much as talking to a white woman.

One of the great attractions of military service in India – one that appealed equally to officers and men, Indians and British alike – was the probability of active service on the North-West Frontier, which providentially remained constantly on the boil, with minor explosions of hostility almost every year and major uprisings every decade or so. Some regiments – notably those in the 'Piffers' (Punjab Frontier Force) – specialized in the highly skilled techniques of frontier warfare, while other regiments took turns at frontier duty, learning the necessary skills for survival the hard way. As the casualty figures bear out it was British Infantry, lacking in caution and experience, which took the hardest knocks.

Mr. *Major C.B. Sr.* [Censored]

regrets exceedingly
his deplorable conduct while a
guest at your

Dinner Party

On _last night_.

and humbly craves your pardon
for the breach of etiquette checked in the
adjoining column. *(Reverse)*

High Cockalorum being played on Mess Night, *c.* 1930; the idea was that one team would pack itself into a tight scrum against the wall while opponents attempted to break it up by jumping on it. *Above centre and right*: an apology card from the 1930s; a vogue that never quite caught on.

Dining-room of the officers' mess, Madras Sappers and Miners, where officers and their (male) guests dined in full mess dress, surrounded by trophies and the regimental silver. The officers' mess was the inner sanctum of the regiment, a jealously guarded refuge complete with totems, rites and taboos.

Regimental wrestling match, *c.* 1890. Although British officers were forbidden to take part in games that involved close physical contact, their zest for sport played a key role in bringing together officers and men in Indian regiments.

........Striking host with bottle.	.........Weeping.
........Spanking female guests.	.........Nausea.
...✗...Inebriation.	.........Excessive destruction of Furniture.
........Breaking china and glasswear.	...✗...Looking for hidden mole
........Complete loss of equilibrium.	...✗...Singing ribald songs.
...✗...Indiscreet petting.	.........Insisting on telling naughty stories.

Reluctant maidens: a group of young recruits preparing to dance at *dashera*, the Gurkhas' autumn festival, 1931. There was always a close rapport between Gurkhas and British troops, who regarded 'Johnny Gurkha' as being a cut or two above the Indian. From the officer's point of view they were ideal fighting material, being simple-minded, bloodthirsty, good-humoured and supremely malleable.

Jubilee Dinner menu, 1897. The Sikhs and the Gurkhas were always held in high esteem by the British, very largely on account of their stout resistance during the Sikh and Gurkha wars in the early nineteenth century, and the support they gave during the Mutiny.

Above: 'Me and the Taj Mahal', 1925. The British Other Ranker (BOR) had an average tour of five years in India, most of it hidden away in army cantonments outside the larger towns. It required considerable initiative on his part to break out of the barracks and see the 'real' India.

Inset: BORs with fruit-bat, 1924, Secunderabad: typical nineteenth-century army barracks – high-roofed buildings with thick walls and deep verandahs – each capable of accommodating over two hundred men.

Interior of an army bungalow, photographed in the early afternoon during the Hot Weather, with the thermometer standing at 115°F. The blurring is caused by movement of the *punkahs* pulled from the outside by much abused *punkah-wallahs*. Wheeler Barracks, Cawnpore, 1932; named after the gallant but foolish General Wheeler, whose action, in handing over the fort to Nana Sahib, led indirectly to the massacre of 1857.

'Do's and Don'ts' for the BOR in the late 30s, produced not from official sources, but by a cigarette manufacturer.

Far right: one of the great institutions of the British Army in India: the regimental *nappi* (barber), who made a circuit of the barracks at dawn with his shaving equipment and hot water, shaving men while they slept.

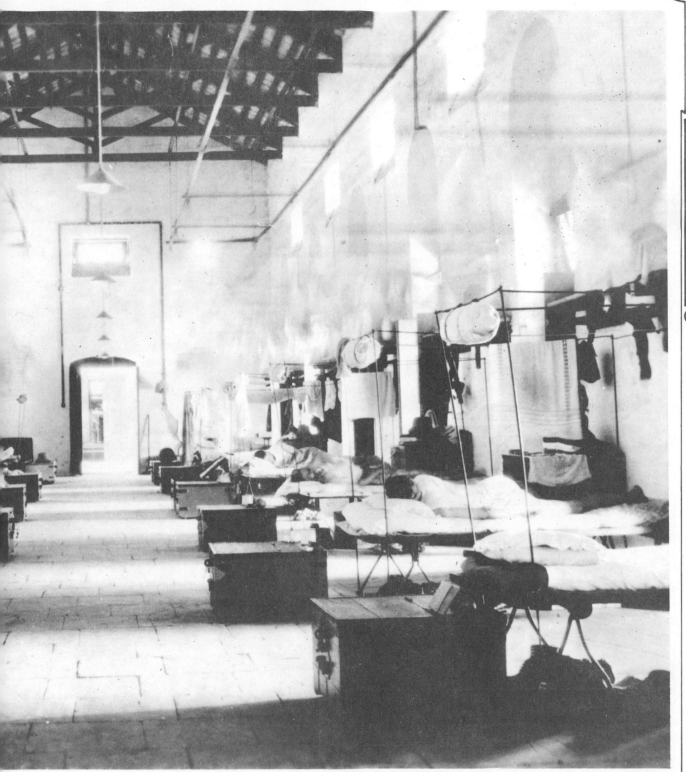

Ferns from Private Cawthorne's scrapbook, collected in the Himalayas in the summer of 1888. Regiments took it in turn to send detachments up to the army hill stations during the Hot Weather. Provided they could save enough money it was also possible for BORs to take local leave and stay at one of the Soldiers' Homes set up in the hills by charitable or religious bodies.

Army Temperance Association, Roorkee, 1901 and temperance medal. Great efforts were made to discourage the heavy drinking that was the great scourge of the British Army in India in the nineteenth century. Although taken perfectly seriously, temperance was more honoured by default than anything else. Troops tended to divide into those who frequented the 'wet' canteen and those who went to the 'dry' one.

'Out of Bounds', Madras, c. 1920: a comprehensive list of areas closed to the BORs. After much campaigning by English moralists in the 1890s army

Regimental concert party, Cawnpore, 1935; and army football match poster, 1931. With time hanging very heavy on their hands the troops were encouraged to play as much sport as they could – principally football (the all-India Durand Coup was the major inter-regimental competition), hockey (frequently against unbeatable Indian sides) and athletics.

1st ARM'D CAR COMPANY, R. TANK CORPS

PRESENT THE

HOT DOGS

CONCERT PARTY (R.T.C.)

IN RAPID FIRE ENTERTAINMENT

IN THE

LORD ROBERTS SOLDIERS HOME

Monday March 25th 1935
8-30 p.m. sharp.

If you are Homeward Bound,

IT IS TIME TO OVERHAUL YOUR KIT.

We Supply

CABIN TRUNKS	BRIEF BAGS
SUIT CASES	KIT BAGS
ATTACHE CASES	HOLDALLS
DRESSING CASES	SOILED LINEN BAGS

ETC.,   ETC.,   ETC.

ALL BRITISH AND BEST.

APESCO GENERAL STORES,

THE MALL, CAWNPORE.

SOCCER DE PAR EXCELLENCE

Watch Regimentals at Play and
be present to Cheer Victors of

Indian Football Shield Test (Hayman Shield)

Unique unprecedented unequalled most
thrilling "Footer" Drama staged
this side of India

FOLLOW THE CROWDS TO THE

FINAL GAME

AT

Ferozeshah Kotla opposite Delhi Jail

On Wednesday the 18th March, 1931
AT 4-30 P.M.

Come one, Come all, Man, Woman and Child
and enjoy yourselves to the top of your bent.

TEA, CAKES and WHISKEY etc in affluence

Miss not, repent not.

Army Press, Delhi.

brothels were officially prohibited, although commanding officers frequently made discreet but strictly unofficial arrangements for their men.

List. Bounds. Madras.

Extracts from station standing Orders and station Orders published from time to time.

The following areas are permanently "OUT OF BOUNDS" to all other ranks except as stated below in the case of George Town only :—

(1.) The whole of the area North of the China Bazaar Road, Evening Bazaar Road, Erusappa Maistry Street, and that portion of General Hospital Road between Evening Bazaar Road, Wall Tax Road, and which is bounded on the West by the Buckingham Canal (inclusive) and on the East by the Indian Ocean, except to those N. C. O's and men who are in possession of a pass to go to the Wesleyan Church in George Town, and with the exception that the following roads are in bounds to full ranks, and to other ranks (below full ranks) when accompanied by their wives:—

(a.) North Beach Road from the East end of the China Bazaar up to the Harbour (inclusive.)

(b.) China Bazaar Road, Erusappa Maistry Street and Evening Bazaar Road.

(2.) CHOOLAI-bounded as follows :—
EAST-by SYDENHAM'S ROAD.
SOUTH-by VEPERY HIGH ROAD.
WEST-by KUNDALLS ROAD.
NORTH-by CHOOLAI BAZAAR ROAD

(3.) NURSINGAPURAM and CHINTADRI-PET, bounded as follows :—
EAST-by RIVER COOUM.
NORTH-by   do
WEST-by   do
SOUTH-by MOUNT ROAD and BLAC-KERS ROAD (exclusive to HARRIS BRIDGE.)

This includes the whole of RIVER SIDE

(4.) TRIPLICANE-bounded as follows :—
NORTH-by Government House Grounds (inclusive)
SOUTH-by Peters Road and Ice House Road.
EAST-by the Marina.
WEST-by Mount Road.

(5.) The following area is permanently placed "Out of Bounds" to troops.
Area surrounding Buckingham and carnatic Mills, Perambur enclosed by and inclusive of the following roads.
COOKES ROAD.
STRAHAMS ROAD.
GANTYS ROAD and the road to the North of the Mills.

(II.) The following places, houses and streets, are permanently "OUT OF BOUNDS" to all other ranks except as stated below against each:—

(a.) ALL RAILWAY STATIONS - including Station refreshment rooms and Bars except to Warrant Officers and to those on duty and those travelling with a pass.

(b.) THE HARBOUR AND DOCKS-except to those on duty and those in possession of a pass signed by an officer.

(c.) GOVERNMENT GENERAL HOSPITAL-except during authorised visiting hours.

(d.) THE ARSENAL TESTING RANGE at FORT ST. GEORGE - situated next to short Ranges near Wallajah Gate.

(e.) THE FORT STABLES ENCLOSURE, the space between the Fort ramparts and the moat, (except in the immediate vicinity of the British Infantry Latrines and 30 yards ranges) and the area enclosed by the wire fencing of the wireless Telegraphy Station.

(f.) House known as "THOUSAND LIGHTS" in Peters Road off Mount Road.

(g.) House known as "PINKIES" No. 8, Banks Lane (behind Minden Club.)

(h.) HOTEL BOSSOTTO'S (late D'ANGELIS HOTEL.) Mount Road except to Warrant Officers and N. C. O's of rank of L./Sgt. and above.

Mounted column 'showing the flag', North-West Frontier, 1931. It was the ambition of almost every soldier in India to see active service on 'the Frontier' or 'up the Khyber', if only to break the monotony of service in the plains. There was always tension on the Frontier, and nearly always hostilities going on in one form or another.

Inset: When the troops transferred from one station to another or went up to the hills in the Hot Weather, they usually did so in the traditional manner, described in Kipling's *Kim*, marching steadily for perhaps twenty days or more, covering some fifteen to twenty miles a day and setting up camp every night. Gruelling as the route march was, it was an experience that most British troops savoured.

Alexandra Piquet, near Razmak, the highest outpost in the British Empire and the scene of a minor disaster in 1935 when a punitive colum was ambushed and besieged by Waziris, suffering heavy casualties.

The North-East Frontier: officers examining arms – mostly flintlocks – seized during the Chin Hills expedition of 1891 (the officer on the left is wearing a Pathan *poshteen* and has probably seen service on the North-West Frontier); *Far right*: a casualty – most probably a victim of malaria – being carried in a *doolie*.

Third Afghan War, 1918-19, with Political Officer and interpreter meeting an enemy deputation bringing goats as gifts. Most operations were concluded after the punitive expedition had lost a few casualties from sniping, made one or two attempts to engage an elusive enemy and blown up a couple of villages. The Political Officer would act as a go-between, deputations would meet under a flag of truce, a *jirga* (tribal council) would be held and fines levied. In a year or two the process would probably have to be repeated.

114

Frontier pass, Malakand, 1938. The North-West Frontier provinces bordered on unadministered tribal territory where such traditional enemies of the British as the Afridis and the Mohmands lived in security, venturing out occassionally on raiding parties which led, in turn, to punitive expeditions.

Not transferable

Pass to :—

MALAKAND
CHAKD'ARRA

Available for _____ 1-2-38

Name ___ Captain & Mrs Cotton ___

for Political Agent,
Dir, Swat and Chitral.

DATED MALAKAND :
The 31-1-38, 193

[P.T.O.]

INSTRUCTIONS.

1. This Pass should be handed in to the Levies at the Road Barrier at Dargai.
2. This Pass does not allow the holder to leave the vicinity of the main road nor to proceed more than 800 yards beyond the limits of the Fort, and visitors must be on the Mardan side of Dargai before sundown.
3. This Pass does not include permission for shooting or fishing.

15

Curzon's Durbar: Lord Lytton's proclamation Durbar of 1877
was a modest affair by comparison with the Durbar of 1903,
which was supposed to mark the accession of King Edward
VII but became very much a celebration of Lord Curzon's
Viceroyalty. A third Durbar in 1911 marked the accession of
King George V as well as the official transfer of the capital
from Calcutta to Delhi.

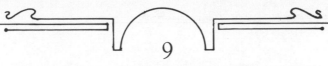

9

High Noon: The Raj in Excelsis

The pomp and the splendour of the Raj were a true blending of east and west, combining Mogul ostentation with British respect for doing things properly. The Mogul custom of the durbar (court or levée) continued to be used at all levels. Its most common form was in the parade of visitors and petitioners that every official would find outside his office or on his verandah every morning, but its most splendid manifestations were to be found, naturally enough, at the Viceroy's court, in the various levées, investitures and social gatherings that were held throughout the year. In 1877, 1903 and 1911 three great Durbars were also held outside the walls of the old Mogul capital at Delhi, where magnificent displays of imperial pageantry revealed the Raj at the height of its powers.

Adding greatly to the colour of all such occasions were the uniforms and costumes worn by the male participants, the Indian princes dripping in jewellery, pearls and silks and the various services with their own distinctive uniforms. The most glamorous were certainly those worn by the cavalry officers, with Indian *puggarees* (turbans), *kurtas* (long jackets) and *cummerbunds* (waistbelts), and *jodhpurs* (breeches) worn with English boots, epaulets and pipings. No Ruritanian uniform could ever outdazzle that worn by the officers of Probyn's Horse – scarlet and gold *cummerbund*, worn over a dark blue coat edged with gold, striped gold and turquoise *puggaree* – or match the famous mustard-coloured uniform of Skinner's Horse.

To a land that made much of its festivals and *pujas* (ceremonies) the British added quite a few of their own. The first of these was the New Year's Day parade, first held in 1877, which opened every year with a burst of military splendour, with massed cavalry and infantry marching and galloping across every parade ground or *maidan* in British India. During the Cold Weather months every station would hold its 'week' and there would be gymkhanas, polo matches and other sporting tournaments – such as the Kadir Cup for hog-hunting, held on the alluvial flats outside Meerut in March – most of which came to an end with the start of the Hot Weather. The dates for these 'weeks' depended largely on the circuit traditionally followed by the Viceroy but in upper India were also arranged to make the most of the weather. Thus Calcutta Week came in January, Delhi Week was in February, Rawalpindi Week in March.

Once the Hot Weather had begun public functions all but came to a halt in the plains but continued unabated in the various hill-stations to which provincial governments transferred themselves. From May onwards every hill-station, from Murree to Mahableshwar, blossomed into vigorous life, although the main magnet for Anglo-Indian society was always Simla, chiefly because it was the summer capital for both the central as well as the Punjab government.

With the coming of the Rains the hills were abandoned and in due course the Cold Weather season began again, with its Thursday 'tea-dances' and Saturday night club dances and fancy-dress balls, reaching its climax with the *burra din* (big day) of Christmas, often celebrated under canvas in jungle camps and with Father Christmas appearing mounted on an elephant or a camel.

Imperial pomp: British India seen at the peak of its greatness – *right*, the King-Emperor's Parade, held on every New Year's Day, and *left*, the Viceroy and Vicereigne enthroned on an elephant, moving in procession to review the Durbar of 1903.

118

A retinue fit for a prince: the Governor of Bombay, Lord Brabourne, and staff, in 1937. The Prince of Wales was reported to have said that he had never realized what royalty really meant until he came to stay at Government House, Bombay, in 1921.

Organized slaughter for visiting dignitaries; a favourite means employed by princes to entice and bring influence to bear on senior servants of the Raj. The Maharajah of Jashpur with the Governor of the central provinces, Sir Montague Butler, and entourage, together with 527 duck.

CHRISTMAS 1923

COMMANDER IN CHIEF'S CAMP
INDIA.

The Christmas camp was a high point in Anglo-India's cycle of events. The wild boar on the Christmas card was painted by the Commander-in-Chief, Lord Rawlinson.

120

The more westernized Indian princes also had their Christmas weeks. Some, such as Bikaner, turned the occasion into a highly organized series of events dominated by shoots and competitions during the day and dances by night.

CHRISTMAS CAMP, BIKANER, 1931.

GENERAL INFORMATION.

1. The Information Bureau is situated in a tent at the north of Guests Block No. 2 at Lallgarh, and in the Inner Garden at Gajner. Please apply there for any information required, or for any lost property.

2. Arrangements for posting letters and sending telegrams are also made in the same Office. There are Post and Telegraph offices in the Palace grounds in Lallgarh and Gajner.

3. Please send your servants to the Tea Pantry near the West Entrance Gate of the Palace at Lallgarh and the Tea Pantry near Kitchen at Gajner for your early morning tea. If you should require your afternoon tea in your rooms this can be had from the same place. For any other refreshments which you may require in your rooms please send your servants to the Pantry at the back of Lallgarh Main Palace and to the Pantry in Lall Niwas at Gajner.

4. If you wish to visit any place in Bikaner, or do anything not shown in the programme, please ask at the Information Bureau for the arrangements you require to be made.

5. Tennis, Squash Rackets and Croquet can be had at any time ; and Roller Skating is available in the evenings at the Victoria Memorial Club.

6. It is requested that unnecessary luggage should not be taken to Gajner. Any luggage left behind at Lallgarh will be carefully looked after ; but your rooms should be carefully locked up.

7. At Gajner short coats are worn for dinner ; and Shikar and Tennis kit during the day time.

8. Transport for your luggage to go to Gajner will be at your rooms at 9-00 A.M. on Sunday, the 27th December, 1931. This will go with your servants by Special train, leaving Lallgarh Palace Siding at 10-30 A.M., and will arrive at Gajner at 12-00 NOON.

9. Guests are requested to have all their luggage ready in good time, as the departure of the special train cannot be delayed ; otherwise the arrangements for Lunch, etc., at Gajner will be upset. Any luggage which cannot be got ready in time will have to go by train on the following day.

10. The start for Gajner will be from Lallgarh Porch by Motor Cars.

11. *It is particularly requested that Guests, wishing to go for walks at Gajner, should not use the road through the Deer Forest past the Outer Tennis Courts and beyond, as this is not only likely to disturb the game, but is also dangerous on account of Wild Boars, and also in case of any rifle shooting going on at the time. They are similarly requested not to use the road round the Lake.*

12. Guests are also requested not to go on the Lake at Gajner as this disturbs the Duck.

13. At every shooting place Guests will find a depôt where cartridges will be available in the event of anyone running short, and where an armourer will repair minor damages to guns on the spot.

14. Whilst driving in cars, *Guests are requested on no account to load their guns or rifles.*

15. It will assist the Bikaner State Railway Authorities if Guests will give early intimation of their requirements for departure. Their task will be facilitated if this is done through the Information Bureau ; and if the approximate time they wish to arrive at their destination is given, their route, timings, etc., will all be arranged for them.

GPB   —12-31—

Durbars of the princes: guests and courtiers in attendance to the young prince of Mysore and his even younger bride, c. 1901. The Maharajah of Mysore acceded to the title in 1895 at the age of eleven. He was a strictly orthodox Hindu who refused to eat with Europeans.

121

Edwardian summer: the Governor's garden party, Naini Tal, 1906. Naini Tal ('Simla seen through the wrong end of a telescope') was quite unlike the other Himalayan hill stations in that it was built round a lake. During the rains of 1880 a landslide hit the Victoria Hotel. While several companies of soldiers were digging out casualties a second landslide came down and engulfed both rescuers and the greater part of the station.

Ranikhet Week, *c.* 1900; and *right*, Rawalpindi Week programme, 1930. All the larger stations had their 'weeks', carefully spread out over the Cold Weather season so as not to clash.

FIXTURES FOR RAWALPINDI "WEEK".

MARCH 1930.

17th March 1930 ...	Monday ...	Club Orchestra. Dancing 6 to 8 p. m. ...	"Retreat" will be sounded on the Club lawn by the Buglers of the 1st K. S. L. I.
18th March 1930 ...	Tuesday ...	Rawalpindi District Military Tournament ...	1st K. S. L. I. Orchestra at Club 6-45 to 8-15 p. m.
19th March 1930 ...	Wednesday ...	Tradesmen's Cup Polo Tournament, 1st Round, (afternoon). Club Orchestra. Dancing 6 to 8 p. m.	The Drums of the East Surrey Regt. will beat "Retreat" on the Club lawn.
20th March 1930 ...	Thursday ...	Club Orchestra. Dancing 6 to 8 p. m. ... Pagal Gymkhana.	Royal Signals Pipe Band.
21st March 1930 ...	Friday ...	Tradesmen's Cup Polo Tournament 2nd Round (afternoon) Northern India Amateur Rackets Tournament. Club Orchestra. Dancing 6 to 8 p. m.	
22nd March 1930 ...	Saturday ...	Races, Spring Meeting 1st day. Northern India Amateur Rackets Tournaments. Dinner and Fancy Dress Dance at Club.	Pipes of 2-17th Dogra Regt.
23rd March 1930 ...	Sunday ...	Special Lunch at Club.	East Surrey Regt. Band at Club 12-15 to 1-30 p. m.
		Cricket. Owners, Trainers and Jockeys, Vs. Patrons, Stewards and Officials Northern India Amateur Rackets Tournament	Royal Signals Pipe Band.
24th March 1930 ...	Monday ...	Tradesmen's Cup Polo Tournament Semi-Finals. Northern India Amateur Rackets Tournament Championship Dog Show in Lansdowne Gardens Club Orchestra. Dancing 6 to 8 p. m.	Military Torchlight Tattoo 9-30 p. m.
25th March 1930 ...	Tuesday ...	Races Spring Meeting, 2nd Day. Performance by Rawalpindi Murree, A. D. S. (Popular Prices). Northern India Amateur Rackets Tournament.	Band of East Surrey Regiment. K. S. L. I. Orchestra at Club 6-15 to 7-45 p. m.
26th March 1930 ...	Wednesday ...	Tradesmen's Cup Polo Tournament Finals. (R. A Rawalpindi "at Home"). Northern India Amateur Racket Tournament. Old Cheltonian Dinner at Club. Ball at Elphinstone Hall in aid of Anglo Indian Children's Relief Association.	East Surrey Regt. Band. The Drums of the Border Regt. will beat "Retreat" on the Club lawn. K. S. L. I. Band.
27th March 1930 ...	Thursday ...	Morning. Great North of India Horse Show. Races Spring Meeting 3rd Day Northern India Amateur Rackets Tournament Club Orchestra. Dancing 6 to 8 p. m. Performance by Rawalpindi Murree A. D. S.	Band 2/7th Rajputs.
28th March 1930 ...	Friday ...	Great North of India Horse Show, all day, (I. A. S. C. "at Home"). Northern India Amateur Rackets Tournament. Performance by Rawalpindi Murree A. D. S.	Band of Border Regt. Pipes of 2/17th Dogras.
29th March 1930 ...	Saturday ...	Races. Spring Meeting (last day). Northern India Amateur Rackets Tournament. Dinner and Dance at Club. Cricket. Rawalpindi Club Vs. Kohat, 1st Day Morning only	State Entry of H. E. The Governor. Band K. S. L. I. Royal Signals Pipe Band.
30th March 1930 ...	Sunday ...	Special Lunch at Club. Northern India Amateur Rackets Tournament. Cricket. Rawalpindi Club Vs. Kohat 2nd Day	Border Regt. Band at Cricket Pavilion 12-15 to 1-30 p. m.

Hobson-Jobson; originally a British Army corruption of the cry *'Ya Hasan! Ya Hasan!'* heard during the Mahommedan festival of *Moharram*, the word came to be used to signify Anglo-Indian *argot*, a mongrel language used by both Britons and Indians and assembled in 1886 into a remarkable glossary.

BURRA-BEEBEE, s. H. *barī bībī,* 'Grande dame.' This is a kind of slang word applied in Anglo-Indian society to the lady who claims precedence at a party. [Nowadays *Barī Mem* is the term applied to the chief lady in a Station.]

1807.—"At table I have hitherto been allowed but one dish, namely the **Burro Bebee,** or lady of the highest rank."— *Lord Minto in India,* 29.

1848.—"The ladies carry their **burrah-bibiship** into the steamers when they go to England. . . . My friend endeavoured in vain to persuade them that whatever their social importance in the 'City of Palaces,' they would be but small folk in London." —*Chow Chow, by Viscountess Falkland,* i. 92.

[**BURRA-DIN,** s. H. *barā-din.* A 'great day,' the term applied by natives to a great festival of Europeans, particularly to Christmas Day.

[1880.—"This being the **Burra Din,** or great day, the fact of an animal being shot was interpreted by the men as a favourable augury."—*Ball, Jungle Life,* 279.]

BURRA-KHANA, s. H. *barā khāna,* "big dinner"; a term of the same character as the two last, applied to a vast and solemn entertainment.

[1880.—"To go out to a **burra khana,** or big dinner, which is succeeded in the same or some other house by a larger evening party."—*Wilson, Abode of Snow,* 51.]

BURRA SAHIB. H. *barā,* 'great'; 'the great *Sahib* (or Master),' a term constantly occurring, whether in a family to distinguish the father or the elder brother, in a station to indicate the Collector, Commissioner, or whatever officer may be the recognised head of the society, or in a department to designate the head of that department, local or remote.

[1889.—"At any rate a few of the great lords and ladies (**Burra Sahib** and **Burra Mem Sahib**) did speak to me without being driven to it."—*Lady Dufferin,* 34.]

Regimental ball, 27th Punjabis, 1912. A popular feature at any large dance was the *kala jugga* (black place), a secluded area surrounded by ferns and potted palms where couples might indulge in light flirtation.

It was customary for the gentlemen to 'book' dances with prospective partners, who would note them down on their cards. There were usually some fifteen or sixteen dances, with a buffet somewhere in the middle. Before the Great War waltzes and two-steps were popular and the evening always ended with a gallop. After the war, the two-step gave way to the foxtrot.

It was also customary for bachelors on the station to return hospitality by joining together to give a bachelors' ball. In Simla the wealthier bachelors and grass widowers formed the Order of the Black Hearts and threw extravagant balls – as well as a children's fancy-dress party – that were the high spots of the Simla season. There was also the Gloom Club which gave elaborate 'mourning' parties. Photograph of the Order of the Black Hearts, 1934.

He is not so —— as he is black.

The Grand Master and Knights of the Order of the Black Heart request the pleasure of the company of

Major & Mrs Masou

at a Fancy Dress Revel to be held in the U. S. Club Tennis Court on Monday October 5th at 9.45 p.m.

R.S.V.
The Prelate, Vice

Bachelor's Ball 1928.

February 29

E. D. S.

Allahabad Club.

British India revelled in fancy dress. Lord and Lady Curzon's farewell ball, 1905, with Lady Curzon as Queen Elizabeth, shortly before her death. Anne Butler (on the extreme left) was – together with the daughters of the next Viceroy, Lord Minto – the first woman to ride a horse astride in Simla. It is said that when Curzon heard that Minto was to succeed him, he remarked, 'Isn't that the gentleman who only jumps hedges?'

BORs in more basic fancy dress, *c.* 1925, including one char-*wallah.*

126

GOVERNMENT HOUSE,
NAINI TAL.

July 1, 1933.

DEAR *Nancy*

HIS EXCELLENCY'S Personal Staff will be very glad if you could come to a small Fancy Dress Dance at Government House on Thursday the 6th of July.

His Excellency would be very pleased if you would dine at Government House before the Dance. Dinner at 8.15 p.m.

Yours sincerely,

Arthur Grenfell

FANCY DRESS—

Apache Costume if possible.

R. S. V. P.

A. D. C. in waiting
Government House.

Mrs Kendall

"The Peace-maker"

Mr Fitzwilliam.   Miss Forbes.   Mrs Goodridge.

Amateur dramatics, another popular Anglo-Indian pastime. Probably the finest productions were those put on by the Simla Amateur Dramatic Society at the miniature Gaiety Theatre.

Unveiling of a statue of the late Queen-Empress in a South Indian native state. The Great Queen was 'both the daughter and mother of Empire', declared Lord Curzon, and revered to a remarkable degree by both Indians and Anglo-Indians alike. Few public parks, either in British India or in the native states, were without a statue of *Maharanee* Victoria.

All too familiar patterns of mortality: regimental casualties sustained during the conquest of upper Burma, some two-thirds of the deaths occurring as a result of general sickness and disease. All along the Grand Trunk Road there were small 'marching cemeteries' where those who died of apoplexy or heat exhaustion during route marches were buried. It is worth noting how class distinctions went beyond the grave, those below the rank of colour sergeant failing to get their names on the memorial stone.

128

10
The Long Afternoon: The Decline of British India

And the end of the fight is a tombstone white with the name of the late deceased
And the epitaph drear: 'A fool lies here who tried to hustle the East.'

Rudyard Kipling, *The Naulahka*

To a great many Anglo-Indians India was 'the land of regrets' (Sir Alfred Lyall's famous lament – often attributed to Kipling – appeared in print in 1885). They saw themselves 'linked in the chain of Empire', their lives overshadowed, like Kipling's *Galley Slave*, by 'burning sun and choking midnight, Sickness, Sorrow, Parting, Death'.

Up to the mid-nineteenth century the death rate among Europeans in India had been staggeringly high. In later years the chances of survival improved but medical ignorance remained widespread. The author of *The European in India or The Anglo-Indian's Vade Mecum*, published in 1878, could still assert with apparent confidence that moonblindness would affect people who slept out of doors, to say nothing of paralysis 'produced by the direct action of the land winds.'

Newcomers and infants, in particular, were always vulnerable to such common scourges as *cholera morbus* – known as 'Corporal Forbes' to British troops – or enteric fever (typhoid), as well as such everyday irritants as dysentery and malaria.

As for Sorrow and Parting, it must be said that the British in India accepted with remarkable equanimity that isolation and loneliness in a variety of forms was part of their lot; it was the price that had to be paid to keep an Empire.

Missing from Kipling's list was the element of violence. Victorians could write of 'the magnificent Pax Britannica that enables the solitary traveller to walk unharmed through two thousand miles of country and two hundred millions of people'. They could sleep out at night under a mosquito net on the lawn, knowing full well that this was (in Maud Diver's words) 'the land of the open door'. Yet no people could go on living unassimilated in another people's land and not be aware that, whatever their

motives and whatever benefits they offered, they were, to a growing number of Indians, unwelcome as rulers. The land had shown violence towards them in the past and threatened at times to do so again. This was the shadow under which all the British in India lived out their lives.

The idea of self-government for India had been introduced as long ago as 1833, when Macaulay had declared that when such a time came it would be 'the proudest day in English history'. Despite the efforts of such Empire-builders as Curzon this goal continued to be proclaimed at regular intervals throughout the next century – and yet very little was done about it. All Anglo-India knew that one day *swaraj* (home rule) must inevitably come; what few could accept, even in the 1930s, was the actual relinquishing of power. Their reluctance was understandable, for many sincerely believed that the Indians were not yet ready for it. It therefore became necessary for India to make them go.

In fact, the final loss of will did not come about as a result of Indian pressures. The political climate in England had changed dramatically since the Great War and Anglo-India was now far too far out of step with the liberal sentiments of successive home governments to be allowed to survive.

In March 1947 the great-grandson of the Queen who had just seventy years earlier been so proudly proclaimed *Kaiser-i-Hind* flew in to Delhi to wind up the Raj. India's twentieth and last Viceroy worked swiftly and with courage. Five months later, at the stroke of midnight on 14 August, the Raj came to an end. As Lord Mountbatten signed away his paramountcy the flag that had flown day and night over the shell of the Residency at Lucknow ever since the Mutiny was finally lowered and the flagpole wrenched from its foundations.

Lt Charles Hearsey died in the charge of the 9th Lancers at Killa Khazi in 1878. His father, General John Bennett Hearsey, was one of the great figures of the Mutiny. Another branch of the family, descended from the adventurer Hyder Jung Hearsey and a Jat princess, served by tradition in the 2nd Lancers. When in the 1890s the *Pioneer* newspaper queried the propriety of a 'half-caste' commanding such a distinguished regiment, the senior member of the family travelled some five hundred miles to Allahabad and horsewhipped the editor in his office.

After the Mutiny civilians formed themselves into local units of the Auxiliary Forces (India) to ensure that the European population would never again be entirely defenceless. The Calcutta Light Horse could be traced back to an even earlier crisis when Dutch forces threatened the city in 1759. *Pukka* soldiers were never terribly impressed by these units; one well-known ditty implied that the Bihar Light Horse rode with 'one hand on the pommel, one hand on the saddle'.

The Prince of Wales reviews Mutiny veterans outside the walls of the Residency at Lucknow, 1905. Anglo-Indians never allowed themselves to forget or forgive the Mutiny, an attitude that Indians were quick to copy after the Amritsar Massacre in 1919, when troops fired upon an unarmed crowd of demonstrators, killing 379 and wounding many more.

Death was so common a feature of Indian life that it was regarded with a certain fatalism. It was not unusual to have been breakfasting with a man in the morning and to be burying him at sunset. In the British Army some levity accompanied such proceedings; the cemetery was known as the 'Padre's *godown*' (storeroom) and after the funeral the band played jaunty airs as the troops marched back to barracks.

The two most vital medicines in India were quinine and chlorodyne, the latter a treatment for diarrhoea and dysentery with opium and chloroform as its principal ingredients.

MOURNING.
OUTFITS FOR INDIA.
JAY'S
LONDON GENERAL
MOURNING WAREHOUSE,
247 & 249, REGENT STREET.

The Proprietors of this Establishment, in respectfully addressing themselves to the attention of the Nobility, the Gentry, and the Public, beg leave to renew their thanks for the extraordinary patronage they continue to receive. Every article necessary for a

Complete Outfit of Mourning,

for either the Family or Household, may be had here, and made up, if required, at the shortest notice ; whilst the attendance of competent persons connected with the Establishment upon families of rank, and of every respectable denomination, enables the proprietors or their assistants to at once suggest or supply everything necessary for the occasion, and suited to any grade or condition of the community.

SKIRTS, &c.,

for Widowhood and for Family Mourning, are always kept made up ; and a note, descriptive of the relation of the parties to the deceased, will ensure at any time the proper supply of Mourning being forwarded, both as to quality and distinction, according to the exigencies of the case ; it being needful only to send dresses for patterns, when every requisite will be carefully prepared and chosen to render the appointments complete.

JAY'S
LONDON GENERAL MOURNING WAREHOUSE,

Nos. 247 & 249, Regent Street, two doors from Oxford Street,
London.   114-Lo.

Centre: Missy *baba* and dogs, *c*. 1925; 'Blobs' the terrier caught rabies and was destroyed. His young mistress had then to travel by train up to the Pasteur Institute at Kasauli for a painful series of injections. Fox terriers were always popular among the British, partly because they seemed to stand up to the climate better than other dogs.

Eczeme Creme (Army & Navy). An effective ointment for Eczema and all inflamed conditions of the skin. Soothing and healing, allays all irritation and itching. To be gently smeared over the parts affected night and morning ... jar 1/5 2/9

Diarrhœa Mixture (Army & Navy) as recommended by the Board of Health during the prevalence of Cholera. Useful in all cases of Diarrhœa, bot. 1/5 2/9

'England and Home' always evoked a powerful nostalgia but returning exiles often found the reality to be a far cry from the idealized images.

Oh, to be playing on Grass Courts — *at home!*

IMMEMORIAL lawns—changeless, traditional, ever-green in park or college or old vicarage garden. Frocks and flannels white against riot of colour in herbaceous borders. Copper beech and bee-humming lime and ancient mulberry-tree casting dappled shade over the tea tables. Gracious and home-like, lawn tennis as they play it at home.

And in the fragile, rose-patterned cups of Spode or Chelsea, Lipton's Tea—the tea they drink in the Old Country, and in India, and all over the world. There is no tea to equal Lipton's in fragrance and flavour and in exquisite refreshing quality. For Lipton's are tea-growers themselves—they understand tea as an English gardener understands lawns —and they send it out, fresh from the tea garden to the tea table, here, at home and everywhere.

Lipton's Tea is packed in airtight tins which keep the tea fresh and sweet. Look for the LL Trade Mark on every tin.

TEA MERCHANTS

BY APPOINTMENT TO H.M. KING GEORGE V.

TEA MERCHANTS

BY APPOINTMENT TO HIS EXCELLENCY THE LORD IRWIN, VICEROY AND GOVERNOR GENERAL.

LIPTON'S
YELLOW LABEL
TEA
WORLD FAMOUS FOR QUALITY

TWO OTHER STANDARD BLENDS:
GREEN LABEL (Special Darjeeling) AND RED LABEL.

ON SALE EVERYWHERE.

Sergeants and wives, Landaur depot, 1900, and an advertisement in a regimental concert party programme, the humour concealing a very real deprivation suffered by the BOR in India. Only a limited number of married quarters were available for the troops, most of them going to senior NCOs. Brothels were officially banned in the 1890s, with a consequent increase in VD and homosexuality. Girls from local Eurasian and 'railway' communities provided occasional solace.

Jubbur Feb 24th 189.

My darling little Son.

Isn't this a funny little cow? Papa has just given her to me, so that Mollie can have some nice sweet milk to keep her strong & well, do you like milk? I wish you could have some from Mollie's cow, she is

A mother's letter to her young son, 1889. Separations – children from parents, wives from husbands – were part and parcel of Anglo-Indian life, accepted stoically and with few outward signs of complaint.

PERSONAL ADVT. LONELY SOLDIER WOULD LIKE TO MEET TWO LADIES WITH VIEW TO BIGAMY. REPLY BOX 22 1st A. C. CO.

Bettiah
15th Aug

Dear Mr Edwards,
I thank you for your note. Herewith statements from your Raiyats. I shall be glad to learn what you have to say with regard to them.

Yours truly,
MKGandhi

To

    Mr. Gandhi Maharaj,
      Bettiah.

Maharajjee--Hail Cherisher of the poor.

    We are the tenants of village Katkenwa Tappa Bahas, beloning to the Bettiah Raj. The village isleased to Hardie Kothi. The good and justice that is done to us by the Hardie factory are detailed below hoping our grievances to be redressed.

(1) The factory realises damages at the rate of Rs 3/- per bigha besides our rent.

(2) The Kothi has a garden of its own containing mangoes and Lichis. Every year the Kothi sends some mangoes and Lichis worth 2 annas to 3 annas to every tenant through its Gorait and realises Rs 2/- to Rs 3/- from every tenant for that.

(3) We are forced to grow oats. We are forced to work on the factory land in weeding, speding etc. for which we are paid 2 to 4 pice each. Sometimes the Kothi does not pay anything for that whereas we get 7 seers, as wages and 1 Poa as Jalpan every day from agriculturists.

(4) Those of us who have ploughs have to supply ploughs with coolies for the zirait land of the factory for 2 to 4 days on account of which our own cultivation suffers and are paid 2 to 4 pices for that. Sometimes we are not paid at all.

(5) We pay rents but receipts are not granted to us regularly

(6) If a tenant's father dies he has to pay Rs 4/- for getting his name registered in the place of his dead father.

(7) There was one Bednan Koeri who held 2 bighas of land. After his death his widow was pursuaded to surrender

Indigo planters had an unenviable reputation as exploiters of their *ryots* (tenant farmers). Their fortunes dwindled during the Edwardian era as synthetic dyes took the place of indigo. The final straw came when Gandhi politicized the indigo *ryots* of Bihar. The Mahatma's letter to an indigo factory manager, written on 15 August 1917, accompanied petitions from local tenants setting out their complaints and marked the opening of a campaign that ended exactly thirty years later to the day with India's freedom won.

134

Anti-British rioting: during disturbances in Peshawar in 1930 an armoured car was set on fire and its occupants burnt to death.

British troops come 'to the aid of the civil power' during inter-communal riots in Bombay, 1940. Perhaps the most vexatious task facing the authorities was the problem of inter-communal violence between Hindus and Moslems, interpreted by some as the outcome of British policies of 'divide and conquer' but already endemic long before the British arrived on the sub-continent.

The forbidden Congress party flag captured after a police raid on an illegal political meeting, Agra district, 1930. Eight months earlier Gandhi had initiated the first act of civil disobedience in what was intended to be a non-violent campaign for *swaraj* (home rule).

During the 30s growing terrorism against officials – at its worst in Bengal, where a number of district officers were shot one after the other by students – forced the government to take security more seriously. *Right*: letter to the wife of a District Commissioner, 1939, and *far right*: letter from an officer of the 14th Sikhs to his wife, *en route* to a trouble spot on the North-West Frontier, May 1930. In April the city of Peshawar had exploded into violence which quickly spread to other areas and became a major armed uprising.

CONFIDENTIAL

No 12/39
GOVERNOR'S CAMP,
UNITED PROVINCES.

December 15, 1938.

Dear Mrs. Vernede,

IN connexion with your invitation to His Excellency to Tea and Tennis with you at your house at 3-45 p.m. on Monday, January 16, 1939,

I am writing you to say that, under rules framed by Government for the protection of His Excellency, it is my duty to write on each occasion asking the hosts kindly to satisfy themselves regarding the *bona fides* of all persons admitted to the house or grounds in which an entertainment takes place which will be attended by His Excellency

The Superintendent of Police continues to be responsible for the protection of His Excellency even when His Excellency is the guest of a private individual or of a public body He will explain to you his decision as to whether he considers it necessary to employ plain clothes men on this occasion, and if so, how many and on what duties. He will also, in consultation with you, make arrangements for regular police to control carriage parking, etc.

Yours sincerely,

Mrs. Vernede,
Collector's House,
Benares.

Major,
Military Secretary

COPY forwarded to Kazim Raza, Esqr., I.P., Superintendent of Police, Benares, for information and necessary action, please.

Sd. D.A. Brett,

Major,
Military Secretary.

1ST BN THE SIKH REGIMENT,
(KING GEORGE'S OWN.)

Nowshera.
Monday
26 May. 30

My darling

A hurried line. Am in Nowshera,
passing through: & spending an hour
here en route to Charsadda & by motor
lorry.

The mess garden is completely bare
not a leaf: & hardly a blade of
grass. My poor rose garden is
pathetic. All done by locusts.

A British police officer was stoned
to death yesterday by the mob, in
Mardan of all places. A barbarous
affair.

'How cruel a thing is separation, sir':
farewell to the sahib, with garlands
and stock eulogies inappropriately
couched in the flowery language of
the Mogul court.

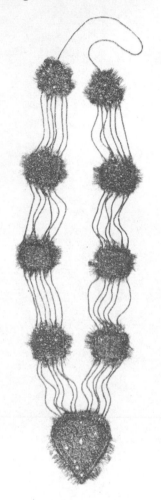

FAREWELL ADDRESS.

Address presented to **Mr. C. T. Allen.**

Asstt. Manager of Circle, R. D. Gondwara.

Sir,

We the members of the Gondwara circle staff beg leave to approch you
with the following few words, on the eve of your departure from
our midst :—

How cruel a thing separation is, sir, that even the most callous heart
reels under its incessant hammering blows.

All along during our official career as subordinates of yours, we have
found you to be a beacon-light to us and you have, during your short
stay here, helped us in steering clear of dangerous rocks and cross currents,
that so often threatened a moral shipwreck in our lives. Your departure sir,
thus leaves us in a different atmosphere, under a different moral and skilful
pilot, who, as we have ever found, has the expertness to take the steer and lead
us to a safe and prosperous destinatin. However, the darkest cloud has its silver
lining. Our consolation lies in the fact that the void created by your departure,
would be befittingly filled up by your successor Mr.......................................
who with fatherly care would foster the best interest of his subordinates and
tenants, as he had done during his previous short stay here.

A ture and pious European as you are, you have exhibited principles
of virtue and morality free from any religious bious, that have
actually lightened your cares and anxieties of the world and have illumined
many other dark souls. Now, sir, you are going to be separated by hundred
of miles, but distance alone is no barrier as the poet says:—

" Far off thou art but ever nigh
I have thee still and I rejoice,
I prosper circled with thy voice
I can not lose thee though die."

And sure sir, even when the elements to elements conform and the
body becomes food for worms, the spirit of kindness and sympathy
starts up, even in our ashes, and tunes up the feelings of those who stand close
by, leaving behind a memory that can be forgotten.

It is more than true, that words are few when the heart is full, and we
can only pray that you may enjoy your new appointment, and remain
ever glorious in the eyes of the world and ever bright in the eyes of Heaven.

We have the honour to be,

Sir,

KORHA.

Your most obedient servants,

oth October 1925.

Amlas of Gondwara Circle, R. D.

CHELTENHAM SPA

Cheltenham had long been a favourite retiring place among Anglo-Indians. According to Sir John Moore's *Health Resorts for Tropical Invalids*, published in 1881, 'the Cheltenham springs have considerable reputation for relieving the diseases engendered by residence in tropical climates, especially chronic rheumatic affections and the disorders of young females.'

'The tumult and the shouting dies; the Captains and the Kings depart': departure of the last British troops – the 1st Battalion, Black Watch – to leave the new state of Pakistan, September 1947.

Topees overboard: the last Anglo-Indian ritual,
that of throwing overboard one's topee as the ship sailed homeward out of Port Said.

'Bound in the wheel of Empire, one by one,
The Chain gangs of the East from Sire to Son,
The Exiles' line brings out the exiles' line
And ships them homeward when their work is done.'

Illustrations

The author and publishers would like to thank the people and institutions mentioned below for kindly allowing material from their collections to be reproduced.

Where there is more than one picture on a page or spread the credits start with the picture furthest to the left and nearest the top of the page and work down each column.

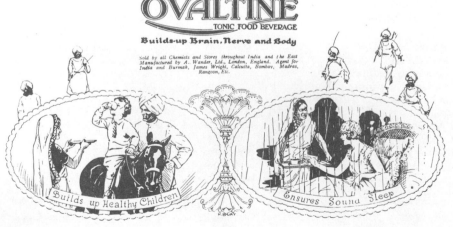